IT'S YOUR MONEY

MONEY

Avoid Costly Mistakes

Denise Winston

Printed in the United States of America
First printing: 2014

ISBN 10: 0-9840581-5-X
ISBN 13: 978-0-9840581-5-0

To every person who has ever felt overwhelmed,
confused, or stressed out about money,
know you are not alone.

Contents

Foreword

Let's face it: Money can be a snore fest, but it doesn't have to be that way—and it shouldn't. Because no matter who you are or where you come from, you will have to deal with money every single day of your life. So let's skip all the technical boring stuff and make it real and relevant to your day-to-day financial life...and even have a little fun.

This book is about you and your money, not me...but if you want to know who I am, where I come from, or how I got to know so much about money, read on; if not, skip to chapter 1.

I learned about money the hard way. Some people may think I look and sound like I've always had it all together—in fact, a lot of people assume I was born with a silver spoon in my mouth—but that's very far from true.

At the age of 16, I was like many young people with a "normal" life: going to high school, getting my driver's license, and dealing with homework, finals, prom, boyfriends, catty girlfriends, and all of the drama that high school brings.

But my home life was—well, let's just say it wasn't normal. I lived in Shafter, California, a small town of only 6,000 people. My mom was in a mental institution and eventually committed suicide, and my dad was off living a double life.

So at 16, I found myself living on my own in Bakersfield, California, a town of 300,000 people, about 20 miles away from home. On top of all of the normal high school stuff, I was living alone in an apartment in a big, scary town, doing my own laundry, grocery shopping, cooking, and cleaning. I was working four jobs, going to school, and handling car issues—and constantly dealing with money. There were no parents around to make me get up in the morning, go to bed at night, go to school, or do my homework. There was no one around to supervise me.

Do you think I made a lot of really good decisions at 16 years old, living in an apartment all by myself? Probably not—but those decisions and life experiences are what made me who I am today, and without them, I wouldn't have written this book and be doing what I'm doing. Out of necessity, I started learning how to handle my money so I could survive—and eventually thrive.

Ever since I was a kid, money has been a hobby of mine (thank goodness). Shortly after I graduated from high school at age 18, I started working at a bank as a teller. I slowly worked my way up, and by the time I was 27, I was a branch manager. I worked at banks for 25 years. It was a great way to see how people handled their money in their day-to-day lives, how the rich got richer and the poor got poorer, and *why*—in addition to how—the banks make their money.

After spending two and a half decades in the banking industry— bursting with financial knowledge, reading one book after another on money, bothered by what was happening to our country with the financial crisis, and tired of being part of yet another bank acquisition (I'd worked for 12 banks in 25 years)—I felt it was time to set out and see how I could use my knowledge and experience to contribute in a meaningful way.

I'd been volunteering in classrooms for about 20 years, at first with Junior Achievement and then with a program I developed over 15 years in the classroom with senior high school students. I designed the program to put better-educated consumers on our streets and into our workforce. I knew from being a banker that when people make better buying decisions at local businesses, it improves our community, state, and nation, and when we have a better-educated workforce, it improves their ability to concentrate on the job at hand instead of their personal financial situation.

My program worked so well that I started getting more and more requests—and now I get to educate people about money full-time by partnering with nonprofits and corporations. I am able to speak to small and large groups of corporate employees, classes of

500 graduating high school students, college students, and many other groups. I've had fun writing books and producing DVDs. I've been interviewed on television more than 100 times, given advice on lots of radio shows, and have been quoted online and in magazine and newspaper articles nation wide.

The best part is knowing that my financial advice has reached more than 100 million people—that what I learned from the hardships of my personal life and the success of my financial career is being put to good use by helping others. My goal is to continue to inspire, empower, and encourage people to take control of their financial lives.

I hope that by reading this book, you'll gain the information and confidence you need to deal with your money—and avoid costly mistakes that can often take a long time to overcome.

Introduction

I*t's Your Money—Avoid Costly Mistakes* introduces you to a new school of thought when it comes to dealing with money. It cuts through all the hype, noise, and get-rich schemes and breaks down what you need to know into bite-size financial snacks that will help you handle your money and avoid costly mistakes. It's based on the knowledge I gained from being a banker for 25 years—dealing with hundreds of thousands of customers, seeing day in and day out how the rich got richer, how the poor got poorer, how the banks made their money—and from my personal experience of living on my own since age 16.

Did you know that most people make between six and ten financial decisions every day? Those decisions add up very quickly. So how you spend your time and what you decide to do *right now* matters! Think about it this way: You can do three things with your time—spend it, waste it, or invest it. Right now you are doing something fantastic: investing your time in your future self.

It's Your Money

Use what you learn from this book to improve the quality of your life and the lives of those around you. Teach others what you know—we need more people like you out there in the world. Together, we're all going to make a big difference!

Let's get started!

CHAPTER ONE

Money Is a Game—Learn the Rules, Play to Win

Somehow most of us have come to believe that true wealth is complicated and reserved for a chosen few, and that the rest of us can only stand by and watch.

Well, forget that.

The truth is we are *all* capable of being rich. We can all do it—it's our right. We live in the United States. Anything is possible!

People get rich by taking advantage of opportunities available to everyone who lives in this great nation. Riches are reserved for those who know and abide by a few simple rules.

Banker's Secret

The typical millionaire is often not the one making a huge six-figure salary or walking around with the high-end label handbag. He or she is the one who understands wealth is not in material things, but in the freedom and choice that wealth brings.

No matter who you are, where you come from, or what your background is, you have to deal with money; it's one thing we all have in common. Money is a fact of life, but don't let it get you down. *Treat it like a game*—and instead of hating the game, learn how to play, and play to win. With the right knowledge, dedication, practice, and choices, you too can become rich.

HOW PEOPLE LEARN ABOUT MONEY

Unfortunately, money is a topic that's rarely taught. Only about 10% of the American population officially learns about it. To demonstrate how the remaining 90% learn how to deal with money, let me ask you a question.

Where did you learn to cross your arms? Hard to say, right? Most people answer, "I don't know…I just did." Some say they learned in church or when they were bored or angry. When I ask people where they learned to deal with money, the answer is almost always the same: "I don't know." Very few people are officially teaching it. Unfortunately, we go to work, get our first paycheck, and start spending…and before we know it, we've developed some financial habits. It's just like learning to cross your arms, and once those financial habits are in place, it can be difficult to make changes. Have you ever tried to cross your arms the opposite way than you normally do? It might feel funny at first, but if you do it often enough, it will come naturally—just like doing something new with money will.

> **People get rich by taking advantage of opportunities available to everyone who lives in this great nation.**

Hopefully, you're reading this book before you start developing any bad financial habits. If not, no worries. No matter where you are in the financial game of life, you will find helpful information in this book.

HOW MONEY IMPACTS US

Having enough money can make us feel smart, confident, successful, and self-reliant. Not having enough money can have a major impact on our lives and cause all kinds of problems. Money is one of the leading causes of divorce in the U.S.—when couples have money issues, they often fight, and it can put stress on their relationship. We also know that financial stress can affect our health, because stress suppresses the immune system, and that can lead to illness. Lack of money affects our self-confidence, too—we can put ourselves down and feel like a failure. Money really has the ability to affect many aspects of our overall quality of life and standard of living.

WHAT HAVING MONEY MEANS TO YOU

Take a moment to think about this: What does money *really* mean to you?

❏ Freedom
❏ Power
❏ Success
❏ Security
❏ Independence
❏ Or (fill in the blank): _____

Knowing what money represents to you helps you stay in the game and keep focused on your goals.

HOW MUCH MONEY DO YOU WANT?

When a person says they want to be "rich," what do they mean? To a young person, being rich may be to have $1,000 or $10,0000 in the bank, and to an older person, it might be to have $100,000 or $1,000,000 or even $100,000,000.

Whichever example you choose, in order to reach your goal, you first have to master the ability to save or make small amounts of money before you can learn to save or make larger amounts of money.

Once you know what you want, it's time to set out and get it. In order to do that, you need to set a goal so you can get it in the most effective and efficient manner. It's just like using a GPS in your car: You punch in where you want to go, hit Enter, and get turn-by-turn directions with time estimates along the way. Would your GPS ever say, 'You want to go where? What are you, crazy? You'll never make it there! Who do you think you are?" Of course not. So don't do this to yourself. Watch the conversion in your head. Anything is possible if you know where you want to go and are willing to do the work to get there.

The simpler and more specific your financial goals are, the better. If you have too many goals or your goals are too complicated and confusing, you run the risk of never reaching them. So start with a small financial goal, master that, then move to the next level.

GET WHAT YOU WANT: SET FINANCIAL GOALS

Let's say I want to buy a new cell phone, and the phone costs $200.

- Goal: $200 to buy new cell phone
- By when: I want to have the phone in 3 months
- How much needed per day, week, month, or year: $200 divided by 3 months = $67. I need to save $67 per month.
- Options to do this: I can earn more or spend less (get a part-time job, sell stuff on eBay, use coupons, reduce or cut eating out, etc.)

Okay, your turn. What's one of your financial goals?

Let's set a goal together right now and figure out how you can get what you want.

❏ Goal: I want to have $ _____ so I can _____.
   (You fill in the blanks: I want x amount of money so I can buy
   a new computer/car/home, get out of debt, take a vacation, quit
   my job, have an emergency reserve, retire, be rich, etc.)

❏ By when: _____

❏ How much needed per day, week, month, or year:

   _____

❏ Options to do this: _____

   _____

Back to the GPS—what does it say when you make an unexpected turn? "Recalculating," right? Well, when you get unexpected money (tax return, bonus, overtime, etc.), recalculate how much you need to save. You can get what you want much quicker by earmarking these unexpected funds.

It's an unfortunate truth that few people set goals, and even fewer create a detailed plan to reach them. Here's the good news: Research shows that when people do the exercise you just did—set clear goals, write them down, and include small steps to achieve them—they are significantly more likely to reach their goals. So congratulations! You've just joined the elite few.

AN HOUR OF YOUR TIME

How much is an hour of your time worth?

Seriously, this is a really important question because when you know that number, it can literally change the way you deal with money for the rest of your life.

It's really easy to figure out: Look at your pay stub and divide your net pay by the number of hours you worked for the pay period. If you're self-employed, it's a bit more complicated, but worth the effort to calculate.

When you know this number, it will help you make decisions about how you spend your time and money. Want that new pair of shoes? You will have to work x number of hours to pay for them. Want to go out to dinner? That will take x hours of work.

So many people tell me they don't have time to use coupons, look for a better price, or find a better rate on a loan. But when I tell them that they could save $10 in 10 minutes by doing a little research, it changes the conversation because saving $10 in 10 minutes equates to $60 an hour. One couple spent an hour identifying a mistake they were making eating out, and saved $400 a month—that's almost $5,000 in one year—by using only two of my tips in just one section of this book. I'll bet you can avoid a lot more mistakes and save even more!

BOTTOM LINE

When it boils down to it, money is really just a tool we can use to live and enjoy life. The trick is to have enough to be rich by your own standards, not get sucked into the trap of thinking money is the be-all and end-all, and resist the temptation to buy more than you need or can afford and give up your freedom. One of the easiest ways to get what you want is to set a goal and figure out how you are going to get there, then take action.

CHAPTER TWO

Work—Make More Money at Work

Most people work for their money (either for themselves or for a company), but there are seven other ways to get money:

1. Inherit it
2. Marry into it
3. Win it
4. Invest for it
5. Break the law for it (steal, deal, or con)
6. Receive it as a gift (from family, friends, government, school)
7. Receive it as a loan (from family, friends, government, school)

Let's take a quick look at these ways. Very few people inherit, marry into, or win money. (Did you know that for 90% of the people who win the lottery, almost all the money is gone within two years? Why? Because they don't have the knowledge or experience to deal with it.) It's hard to invest to make money if you don't have it, and luckily very few people are willing to break the law for it.

> **Make work your best friend—it can buy you freedom.**

Then there are the last two ways of getting money, which are forms of financial assistance—public, family, or otherwise. Here's the issue with being given money: It often comes with control.

Take my daughter, Brandi, for example. When she was a teen and I was paying for her cell phone, what did that give me the right to do? Well, it meant she was at my mercy—I could control everything about the phone. I could take it away, say when it could be used, and it would have given me the right to see anything and everything that went on with that phone, right? (By the way, she hated that—and as soon as she could pay for her own plan, she did!)

MAKE WORK YOUR BEST FRIEND

So that leaves us with having to work for our money. When you go to work and clock in on the job, you're literally trading your time for money—a paycheck. Earning potential is one of the most compelling factors for people when deciding on a career path. Spending a little time choosing the right field in a stable industry can pay off BIG-TIME. If you want to know how much people are making in any industry so you can figure out where to hone your skills, check out sites like **payscale.com** and **salary.com**.

Once you've chosen a stable industry and have the necessary knowledge, skill, certification, or degree, and put yourself close to jobs in that field, it's time to get the best job.

 There's a place for every single one of us in this world; we each have a given talent. The key to success is to figure out what you're good at, what you love to do, and how you can be most helpful. No one is better than anyone else—we each bring something different to the table. It takes all types to make this world go around. Successful companies need all kinds of people: computer programmers, salespeople, logo designers, ad campaign teams, project managers, and a gazillion others.

HOW TO EVALUATE JOB OFFERS

Regardless of whether you're new to the job market or have been working for years, one of the smartest things you can do is to carefully evaluate job offers. Money just might be hiding right before your eyes in the form of *perks*.

Example:

Would you prefer...

Job A for $50,000/year or Job B for $54,000/year?

At first glance, you'll probably want to choose Job B because it looks like more money.

But how much money could be *hiding* in this job offer? $12,064 a year!

	Job A	Job B
Salary	**$50,000/yr.** **($24.04/hr.)**	**$54,000/yr.** **($25.96/hr.)**
Pension (10%)	$5,000	
401K Match (3%)	$1,500	
Medical Contribution	$3,000	
Dental Contribution	$720	
Life & Disability Insurance	$100	
Vacation Time	$1,923	
Sick Time	$961	
Paid Education	$2,500	
Gym Membership	$360	
Value	**$66,064** **($31.76/hr.)**	**$54,000** **($25.96/hr.)**

You can see that Job A offers much more value when you add in the extensive list of benefits like health insurance, dental insurance, 401(k) (retirement) match, sick time, vacation time, and continuing education. Often money can hide right under your nose in disguise.

 Don't Be This Guy!

I had one employee who worked for the bank for 10 years. He made a decent hourly wage and had full benefits like the ones in the example I gave for Job A. He came to me one day to let me know he was quitting because he found another job that paid more. He said he'd be making $0.50 more per hour and needed the money. When I asked how the benefits were, he said there weren't any…and he was okay with that because he'd be making that $0.50 per hour more. When you run the numbers, $0.50 for 40 hours a week equals $87 per month, which is $1,040 per year—but he walked away from well over $10,000 per year in benefits! If he had played his cards right, he could have easily earned a raise (see how to get a better raise later in this chapter). That was a very expensive shortsighted decision on his part.

YOUR PAYCHECK: GROSS VS. NET

Okay, now that you have a job and the money is coming in, it's time to take a close look at your paycheck.

Here's what typically happens: You go to work. You work your regular shift of 40 hours, plus let's say you also work five hours of overtime that week. For easy math, let's say you make $20 per hour. So 40 hours x $20 = $800, plus five hours of overtime at $30 is 5 x $30 = $150. So you're thinking your check should be $950 for that week.

Here's what's "gross" about the situation: After taxes and deductions, that $950 literally gets cut by about 30 percent, so instead of seeing $950 in your paycheck, you only see a net paycheck of $665.

Now it's your turn. Let's take a look at your paycheck. Fill in the blanks below with your actual paycheck numbers:

Gross Pay (before any deductions): $_____

Net Pay (after taxes, insurance, and other deductions):
$_____

Bonus Extra-Credit Calculation: How much do you actually take home *per hour*? Knowing this will help you make a lot of decisions in the future. For example, the next time you want that new $150 pair of shoes, you may quickly change your mind when you realize: *I'll have to work x number of hours to pay for them.*

It's easy to figure out your hourly take-home pay. Take your net pay and divide it by the number of hours you worked for that pay period.

Net Pay $ _____ divided by hours worked _____
= _____ this is how much you have to spend for each hour you work

 Don't Be This Guy!

Unfortunately, I've seen way too many people who thought they made an additional $100 and bought something in advance, only to get their paycheck and realize their deductions were significant and they didn't have the money to pay for what they bought AND keep up with their regular bills. So they reached for a credit card and went into debt...or even worse, they did payday loans or had to pawn things they owned, like their car…seriously! I knew a guy who literally had to pawn his car to cover his rent until he got paid. Don't be that guy. NEVER spend your paycheck before you get it, and always do the math so you don't find yourself in over your head.

HOW TO GET A BETTER RAISE

Once you get a job, one of the smartest things you can do is to figure out how to get a better raise. This one strategic money power play will pay you year after year after year. Any time you can make your boss's job easier, it's a good thing.

Usually raises only come around once a year. However, not all companies give raises every single year. Even if they don't, following a few simple steps will show your initiative and help you stand out. That way, the next time you want to apply for a new position or a promotion becomes available, you'll shoot to the top of the candidate list.

 Banker's Secret

I was a bank manager for many years and I did hundreds of employee reviews. I can tell you that employee reviews/ evaluations are very labor-intensive for management. I had to do them on top of my regular duties and received very little training on how to do them, and it was very stressful. So help your boss give you a good review.

Make sure you're never overlooked for a raise. Here's how to do it.

- ☐ **Time it right.** Generally salary increases and budgets are allocated to management at the end of the year. In January, management gathers information, evaluates your performance, stack-ranks employees, and decides who gets a raise and how much. Then in March or April, your boss will sit down, show you what your review looks like, and, if you're getting a raise, how much that raise will be. By then it's too late to negotiate getting a raise.

- ☐ **Prove your worth in advance.** In January, start keeping an accomplishments or "good stuff" folder, as I like to call it. Make a folder to keep somewhere at work or at home, and in it, put anything and everything good that you do during the year. If your boss gives you a compliment that you handled a customer situation well, make a note for your folder. If your boss sends you an email about a job well done, print it and put it in the file. If you're selected to head up a fundraising team, put it in the folder along with how much you raised (bosses love numbers). If you're selected for a special project, or to lead it, then note that in the folder. If you volunteer to mentor someone, put it in the folder. Every January, when it comes time to prove your worth, you'll have everything you need to complete the final step.

❏ **Help your boss give you a good review and raise.** Go to your boss and say something like this: "I'm so excited about this year's review. Last year was incredible—I've put together a couple of talking points for my review." Then hand him or her the list you've compiled from your good stuff folder. Of course, your boss will have standard information that he or she tracks, like your days absent, specific goals he or she has set for you, and stuff like that. The information you put together from your good stuff folder will allow you to shine. Trust me, very few people in your office, if any, will do this. This will give you the advantage to secure your best raise.

 Don't leave money on the table at work. Take the time to fully understand your benefits. Make sure you look for a 401(k) plan company match, employee discounts, matching gifts, employee education reimbursement, and other perks.

BOTTOM LINE

Work done well does a person good. Careful planning of higher education in a stable industry is important to build your most valuable asset—YOU—and your earning potential. Once you're in an industry, it doesn't have to stop there. You can increase your ability to make money by attending industry seminars, earning certificates, or getting an advanced degree that's in demand in your field. It will help you stand out. The more we learn, the more we can earn. *Investing in yourself is the most important investment you can make.*

CHAPTER THREE

Save—Protect Your Future

S aving your money—10% or more—is one sure way to protect your future.

Quick example: Let's say I'm an egg farmer (I'm a country girl, by the way, raised in a small farming town, and I was a member of Future Farmers of America in high school), and every day I collect 10 eggs from my chickens. I gather those  eggs, put them in my basket, and only use 9 of them—I keep one for myself. If I do this every day for 30 days—collect 10, use or spend 9—there's no possible way that my basket won't be full at the end of 30 days. Granted, during the month, I'm going to have to protect that basket of eggs and make sure none of them get broken, are stolen, or become rotten. But if I consistently follow that plan—collect 10, spend 9, saving 1 egg every day—the basket will be full at the end of every month. After a few months I will have so many eggs I will need to do something with them. Ideally I will incubate them so they hatch into chickens and ultimately lay more eggs (see chapter 9 on investing).

It works the same way with saving money. If every month, out of every paycheck, you save at least 10% of what you earn for yourself, one day your basket will be overflowing, just like the egg farmer's. You will have enough saved to live on if something happens, and after a while you will have so much excess, it will be time to do more than save; it will be time to invest. You work hard for your money—there's no reason to give every single penny away. It's your right to keep some for yourself.

> **A portion of everything you earn is yours to keep.**

WHY SAVE MONEY?

Why save money when it's so easy to spend it all?

☐ **Things happen.** When my daughter, Brandi, was 21 and working as a physical therapist's aide, she was driving to work and got a speeding ticket. Guess how much that speeding ticket cost? Two hundred and seventy-five dollars, and if she didn't want it to go on her driving record (which would increase her insurance rate), she'd have to go to driving school on top of that, which costs another $98. That's a total of $373. Now if she didn't have that money in a savings account, she'd have to put both the ticket and driving school on a credit card. And if she only made the minimum payment on that credit card, it would take her more than two and a half years to pay it off, and it would cost her an additional $100 in interest. Not good!

☐ **People get sick.** It's also important to save for the unexpected. Take me, for example. A few years ago, I had appendicitis. Did I do anything wrong to get that appendicitis? Nope, and going to the hospital emergency room, undergoing a bunch of tests, staying overnight, and having the surgery was really expensive—it cost thousands of dollars! Thank goodness I had health insurance, but I still had to pay some of the bills and for my hospital stay, surgery, and medication. On top of the medical costs, I couldn't go to work, so if I hadn't had sick time, I would have lost out on pay, too. Illnesses cause major financial issues for many people.

☐ **People get old.** A lot of people say that you need to save for retirement, and you do—however, some people have a hard time seeing themselves retired, so they never save for what they can't see in their mind. So I say what's really important is to save for when you *get old and can no longer work.* You've seen really old people and how hard things are for them, haven't you? How hard it can be for them to sit in a chair, move about, see, and hear? And how they can be sitting in their chair watching a young man working, and know *exactly* how to do the job that young man is doing, but they're not physically able to do that job? THAT is what you need to save for! It's not death you need to worry about. You have to save and plan for your elderly years when you'll no longer be physically and mentally able to work and earn money.

❏ **It feels good.** Saving money provides you a sense of security and independence and helps you create wealth.

 WARNING: *If you don't have money set aside in savings, the likelihood is that you'll reach out to credit to try and get by—and that will cost you dearly in interest, freedom, and peace of mind. You have to create your own world where you are financially independent. Having debt and relying on someone else's money is like having a ball and chain attached to you at all times. It robs of you of your freedom. Having money saved does just the opposite.*

WHEN TO START SAVING MONEY

Start saving TODAY. I mean right now! If you can start saving 10% or more, fantastic! If you can't, then start with 1% or 2% of everything you earn; something is better than nothing. Then each time you get a raise, increase the amount you set aside, and before you know it, you'll be saving 10% or more of everything you earn.

HOW TO SAVE MONEY

❏ **Step One:** Open an account earmarked for emergencies or, as I like to call it, "stuff happens." Do NOT link this account to your regular day-to-day checking account, and do NOT link your ATM card to it. You want this account to be as inconvenient as possible so you're not tempted to spend the money.

You want to basically forget about it, kind of like how you forget about the spare tire in your car.

☐ **Step Two:** Set up a percentage or dollar amount of your net paycheck to be deposited directly into the account each payday. If you cannot set up direct deposit, do it manually when you get to the bank or set up an automatic transfer in your online account. You want to be systematic about it. If you're just starting out and can save 5% to 10% right off the bat, that's fantastic! You don't want to get accustomed to having that money available each month...most of the time we spend what we have. If, however, you're already used to having access to that money, it's best to start with a small amount. If you start too aggressively and try to set aside large amounts right out of the gate, you run the risk of having to withdraw the money, and that defeats the purpose of setting money aside in the first place. It's the habit you want to create—once you get good at it, you can increase the amount. Trust me, this feels really good. Ideally you want to have six to eight months of your net take-home pay in your emergency/stuff happens account. I know that's really hard to do. Too many people say, "I can never do that," so they give up and don't save anything. Don't let that be YOU! Over time you will get there, so start small. You'll be amazed how quickly your money will add up and how successful you'll feel when you have money in the bank to fall back on.

❐ **Step Three:** Set up some kind of retirement account or, as I like to call it, "old age" account. Again, set up direct deposit if you can and put in 5% to 10% of your gross pay (before deductions) this time. If your company has a retirement program and offers a 401(k) match, at the very least put in the amount they will match; it's like free money. The glory of setting money aside pre-tax (before tax deductions) is that if you put $100 in, you'll only feel the effect of about $70 because of how the taxes work. Time is money…money in the right account will accrue interest, and that interest will then earn interest. This is called compound interest. You put $2 or more into the right account, and after a while, with a little bit of care, another dollar will start to form and eventually be born. I call it "making money babies." (See chapter 9 on investing.)

 Banker's Secret

You can get what you want and achieve your goals much quicker by strategically using financial windfalls—use your overtime, bonuses, or tax returns to get a jump-start on your savings plan.

You cannot afford to put this off. It's simpler than it may seem. Don't let being unsure about what type of retirement account or investment to put your money in stop you. If you work for a large company, they will most likely have a support department or team that can help you choose what type of account to put your money into. If it's still too overwhelming, just put it into some kind of money market account until you feel more confident. You can do it!

BOTTOM LINE

Saving makes you feel good, helps you avoid debt, creates wealth, protects your future, and secures your ability to live comfortably when things happen and you get old. Once you start saving, you'll have a few different savings baskets: one for emergencies, one for retirement/old age, and one for wealth. You may even have some smaller baskets for short-term goals like a vacation or a new computer, or a larger basket to save for a car or a new home. When you save money and pay cash to purchase an item, you avoid paying high interest rates and the high cost of impulsive immediate gratification.

CHAPTER FOUR

Budget—Live by the Golden Rule of Spending

A budget is basically a way to keep you from spending all of your money on casual desires and impulse buys, and help you control your expenses.

WHY BUDGET?

Look at it like this. Let's say I live in California and I want to go to New York City. One day, I randomly jump in my car and start driving in that direction. What's the likelihood that I'll actually make it to New York City with no planning? By the time I get 100 miles away from home, I'll probably be lost.

> Live and enjoy life on no more than 90% of what you earn. It's easier than you think.

Now let's say I decided to do a little planning, and I plan for one hour the night before I leave. I pull up a map and see that New

York is roughly 3,000 miles from California. I find out how long it will take me to get there, what routes I should take, what I will see, where I plan to stay the night, and how much it will cost for gas. With just one hour of planning, I've increased my potential of arriving in New York City, right? Let's say I add one more thing to help me: technology—a GPS that will let me know where I am, how long it will be until I get there, and step-by-step directions to get there. Now I've significantly increased my ability and likelihood of arriving in New York City in the most cost-effective and time-efficient way.

Budgeting is like this. If you just get your paycheck and live by the seat of your pants, spending as you go, trust me—you will never have any money left at the end of the month and it will be next to impossible to reach your dream financial destination.

 Banker's Secret

If you don't know what to do with your money, someone else surely will.

HOW MUCH TO SPEND

We're all at different financial stages in life and have different financial destinations. As a young person, your financial destination might be to buy a new computer or a car. As you get older, your goal might be to buy a home, take a vacation, or get out of debt, and as you get even older, it might be to retire early, have a vacation home, or simply to be rich. At different times of life, we'll play the game differently and try to win for different reasons.

Unfortunately, most people never spend an hour or two to plan their financial destination, let alone an hour reading a book on money (good for you!). Just the fact that you're reading this book tells me that you are different and you will reach your financial destination, whatever it is.

The simplest way to break down your earnings into a budget is:

☐ Save 10% or more of your income—it's yours to keep.
☐ Spend 90% and no more of your income to live (pay bills, rent, etc.) and to enjoy life.

HOW TO BUDGET

Figure Out Your Income: It's important to know how much money is coming into your household on a monthly gross basis, and what the net amount is that you have to spend each month after taxes, deductions, and savings. You'll want to use your baseline salary/income when it comes to budgeting and use your net take-home pay for this calculation, because that's the actual amount of money you have to spend after taxes and deductions. Reserve any overtime or bonuses for strategic money power plays: funding your emergency cash reserve, paying down high interest debt, helping with major purchases, or saving for retirement or to create wealth.

Net take-home pay: _____

(hours worked x hourly wage – deductions = net)

x 10% yours to keep: _____

(savings for emergency, wealth, old age)

Net take-home pay – $ yours to keep = _____,

or 90% to live and enjoy life.

Figure Out What to Budget For: Budget for necessities and to pay for enjoyment without spending more than 90% of your income. (See worksheet on next page.)

Start by listing your fixed expenses (rent, car payment, etc.) and variable expenses (utilities, food, etc.). Let's do it right now—it will take less than five minutes. If you're not the person in the household who handles the money, then guesstimate or put an asterisk by anything you have questions about. If you're just starting out or moving from one location to another, you can use a cost of living calculator on a site like **bankrate.com** or **bestplaces.net** to figure out how much things cost.

Housing (rent/lease/mortgage payment, taxes, insurance) $ _____

Electricity $ _____

Gas/Trash/Water $ _____

Internet/Cable/Home Phone $ _____

Cell Phone $ _____

Car Payment/Transportation $ _____

Car Insurance $ _____

Gasoline $ _____

Auto Maintenance/Repairs/Registration $ _____

Groceries $ _____

Eating Out (restaurants, snacks) $ _____

Personal Grooming (haircuts, color, nails) $ _____

Entertainment/Hobbies $ _____

Clothing $ _____

Credit Cards/Student Loans/Debt $ _____

Health (prescriptions, co-pays, gym dues) $ _____

Kids (tuition, activities, daycare, allowance, lessons) $ _____

Child Support/Alimony $ _____

Pets (food, grooming, veterinary) $ _____

Bank Fees/Misc. $ _____

Vacation/Gifts/Charity $ _____

TOTAL $ _____

There are a gazillion different expenses a person could have—the above list is just a place to start. If you're looking for additional resources and really want to get down to the nitty-gritty of your expenses, you can look at your credit card and bank statements. You can look at old bills, and you can go online and find out if you really want to project how much items are going to cost. You can either backtrack to figure it out or simply start tracking today.

 Do a budget at least once per year and EVERY time you're considering upgrading your lifestyle by adding a new expense/payment to your budget (cable, changing a cell phone plan, buying a new car, etc.). Otherwise, you run the risk of spending more than you have, forcing you to go into debt to make up the difference or having to cut back on how much you save...and you worked hard for that money! No reason to give it all away.

People always ask me how much they should be spending on housing, car payments, and stuff like that. Here's how bankers figure it out: They use *debt-to-income ratios* based on your gross income.

In 2014, new guidelines were established allowing a borrower to have a total combined debt/income ratio of up to 43% of their gross income. I highly recommend using the previous standard conventional loan debt-to-income ratios of 28/36 to be safe and not get in over your head:

☐ No more than 28% of your gross income should be spent on housing (rent/lease/mortgage payment, insurance, and taxes).

☐ No more than 36% of your gross income should be spent on housing PLUS recurring debt (auto loans, credit cards, student loans, child support, alimony, etc.).

Here's a simple example of what these expenditures look like:

Yearly Gross Income = $45,000/divided by 12 = $3,750 per month income

$3,750 Monthly Income x 0.28 = $1,050 allowed for housing expense

$3,750 Monthly Income x 0.36 = $1,350 allowed for housing expense PLUS recurring debt *(note that ONLY $300 is allotted in this scenario for ALL recurring debt)*

Use Technology, Automate, and Simplify: You can do an Internet search for "budgeting worksheets" and find some for free, or use a site like **mint.com** for apps or Quicken for full-on budgeting software. Or use one of the oldest and simplest forms of budgeting: pen and paper, or the envelope system—where you put the title of an expense on the outside of an envelope (like "gas" or "groceries"), put your allotted amount of money for the month in the envelope, and when the money is gone, it's gone. Each person has a different way they like to track things, so find the one that's right for you: pen and paper, smartphone app, online budgeting tools, budgeting software, envelope system—it's your choice.

Check Your Numbers: Let's see how closely you estimated your eating out expense. This is a great double check. One girl I did the next exercise with was spending $250 per month on coffee and didn't even realize it. Another couple I worked with estimated their eating out expense at $400 per month, and when we did the next exercise, we came up with a whopping $900 per month!

Here's how it works. In the boxes on the next page, if you spend money on a daily basis in any of the categories, write in how much you spend and the number of days you spend that amount. For example, each week when I'd get up at 4:30 a.m. to do a money-saving segment on TV, I'd stop afterward and reward myself with a cup of coffee; I spent $4 for that coffee, so I put that in the first box. I'd also grab coffee with a girlfriend at least one additional day per week, so I put 2 in the Days Per Week box. Next, I run the numbers: $4 x 2 = $8 goes in the Weekly Amount box. My husband and I would eat out at least 2 nights per week at $40, so I put $40 in the Dinner Out box, 2 in the Days Per Week box, Total for Typical Week $80. If I stop right there and add up the numbers for the month, 2 cups of coffee per week and 2 nights eating out is $352 per month. Yikes! It adds up quickly.

Now it's your turn to see how close your estimate for eating out was:

Daily Spending: Eating Out

Item	Typical Amount	Days Per Week	Weekly Amount
Morning Beverage	$	x	=
Breakfast	$	x	=
Mid-morning Snack	$	x	=
Lunch	$	x	=
Afternoon Snack	$	x	=
Habits (cigarettes, alcohol, etc.)	$	x	=
Dinner	$	x	=
		Total for typical Week	
		x4 Monthly Total	
		x12 Annual Total	

Final Check: Let's see where you stand. Do you have extra money at the end of the month or are you spending more than you're bringing home?

Net take-home pay: _____ *(hours worked x hourly wage – deductions = net)*

x 10% yours to keep – _____ *(savings for emergency, wealth, old age)*

90% live and enjoy life = _____

Your total expenses – _____

Final number +/- _____

It's Your Money

If you have extra money at the end of the month because you're spending less than 90% of your take-home pay, fantastic! If you're spending more than you should be, you can do something about it! Thank goodness you've run the numbers now so you can make adjustments to get yourself back on track.

 Don't Be This Guy!

During one of my corporate workshops, I had one guy who had never run these numbers and couldn't understand why each month he and his wife were getting further and further in debt. When we sat down and ran their fixed and variable expenses, they were $2,000 more than the couple was bringing home each month, but they didn't realize it because they were using a credit card. Before we got a handle on it six months down the road, they were $12,000 in debt because they never stopped to run these numbers.

Remember, you get to make your own financial decisions and that means you're in control. Just know that your largest expenses/payments may pose the toughest decisions and require a temporary adjustment: housing and transportation. You might have to get a roommate, find a smaller place, or downsize your car. However, the most control may lie in your daily spending and variable expenses—and that's good because there are a gazillion ways to save money. (See chapter 10 on everyday money.)

Once a year, track your daily spending for 30 days to see if you've developed any new spending habits. You can easily do this with a smartphone app or by keeping a pen, an envelope, or a small notepad with you to jot down expenses. I like to use an envelope so I can put my receipts inside after I note when I purchase gas, eat out, or buy a cup of coffee or a magazine—and even if I'm shopping online. (Sometimes shopping online doesn't feel like spending money to me!) New habits quickly add up, and doing this once a year helps you see how much that new habit is costing you.

When I was young, I smoked cigarettes, and unfortunately didn't realize when I took the first puff of that cigarette that I was going to become addicted—and how much that was going to cost me over the years. Back then, a pack of cigarettes cost $3 a pack, so smoking a pack a day was costing me almost $1,100 a year! Thank goodness I eventually quit. Not only did quitting save me a ton of money, but it also saved me something much more valuable: my life.

Not establishing a budget/spending plan can be like having termites that eat away at your home without you knowing it. Unfortunately, that's what happens many times with daily spending: It may not destroy you immediately, but over a period of time, daily spending can really have a long-term significant impact on the structure of your financial house.

Track your spending. Tracking your monthly expenses over a 12-month period gives you a huge advantage to accurately project your expenses for next year, and it can absolutely keep you on track.

BOTTOM LINE

Most of the time it's not what you *make*—it's what you *spend* and what you *keep* that matter. Remember to set financial goals and communicate with your partner (if you have one), and it's okay to motivate yourself with rewards and splurge every now and then along the way—just plan for them, and plan for the unexpected, too. Oh, and don't fall for the temptation to buy things to impress people you don't know or even like, for that matter.

CHAPTER FIVE

Banking—Become a Bank Account Genius

I t's important to understand that you will most likely have a bank account for your entire adult life. We need bank accounts to operate in day-to-day life. A bank gives us a safe place to keep our money so it won't get lost or stolen, a convenient way to pay our bills, a place to get loans, and a place to invest our money.

Think like a banker.

When you open an account with a bank, it's the start of a banking relationship that, if all goes well, could last a lifetime. Relationships work best when we communicate well with each other and treat each other with respect, and it's reasonable for both parties in any relationship to benefit.

Banks end up knowing a lot about you—how much money you have, what your spending habits are, what your credit is like—

and they use that information to determine what products and services they should market to you and how much they should charge. Not all banks and bankers are created equal, but the basics of what they do are the same. So it's wise to be an educated consumer and remember that you AND the bank are out to have a profitable relationship; it works both ways.

 You can use your multiple accounts and relationship with your bank as a tool to get products and services for free. Remember, not all bankers and banks are created equal—the people hired by a bank often go through a very limited training program. This is why you must be an educated consumer. Know what your options are and what's available. Ask questions when you're opening a bank account to make sure you're getting the best products and services that meet your specific needs and situation. (See checklist of questions on page 48.)

 Banker's Secret

Banks need to make a profit, and one way they do this is to have a "cross-sell ratio," which means that they will try to sell multiple products and services to every client or household that comes into the bank. Additionally, the banker (new account person, teller, etc.) has a sales goal and usually makes a commission off everything he or she sells.

The bank's strategy is that the more products and services you have with them, the more likely you are to stay. If there should ever be a mistake or problem, it's difficult to close a checking account, savings account, credit card, and mortgage loan, so the bank wants you to have lots of products and services. This can be good for you, the consumer. Know that when you have several products and services with one bank, you end up being a very profitable customer to that bank—and you can work that to your advantage.

HOW TO FIND THE BEST BANK

The best bank is the one that's convenient to you, where you can get a good deal, feel you can trust the place, and feel good about doing business with them. You want the bank to be close to where you live, work, or go to school. You don't want to have to spend money getting there or time waiting in line. You can shop around and compare accounts on sites like **bankrate.com**.

 If you're a student, open your account before you graduate or leave school, while your student ID is still valid. Your student ID may qualify you for a free account, and it counts as a second form of ID. Students often struggle with the second form of ID because they may not have a valid credit card or work ID.

WHAT YOU'LL NEED TO OPEN AN ACCOUNT

If you're trying to open a new bank account, here are the items you will need, per the USA PATRIOT Act: your social security number and two forms of identification—one primary identification, such as a state driver's license, state ID, or passport; and one second form, such as a student ID, employee ID, or credit card.

TEN QUESTIONS TO ASK WHEN OPENING AN ACCOUNT OR EVALUATING AN ACCOUNT YOU ALREADY HAVE

1. **How can I avoid the monthly service charge?** _____
    - ❏ Direct deposit (when your employer automatically deposits your paycheck)
    - ❏ Automatic transfer (when the bank automatically moves money each month from one of your accounts to another)
    - ❏ Transaction requirements (certain minimum of debit, check, or deposit transactions)
    - ❏ Minimum balance (certain account balance at all times)

2. **If there is no way to avoid the monthly service charge, how much will it cost?** _____

3. **Are there services that I can get for free?** _____
    If so, what are they and how can I get them? (Never hurts to ask!)

4. **How much will it cost if I overdraw my account?**

    _____

Overdrawing your account is referred to as non-sufficient funds (NSF). This means that if you spend more money than you have in your account, the bank covers the difference…for a hefty fee! It's like an expensive short-term loan. The NSF fee can be more than $35! (How many hours would you have to work to pay for making that accounting mistake?)

5. **How can I opt out?** _____

When you "opt out," you're telling the bank that when you use your debit card and there's not enough money in your account to cover your transaction, they should decline and refuse the transaction instead of overdrawing your account and charging you the hefty NSF fee described above.

6. **Is there a cost for online bill pay?** _____

Using online bill pay is a great way to save time and money. No more paying for postage! You can set up text and email alerts on your account, and you have access to your information anytime and anywhere, virtually eliminating your need to go to the bank.

7. **How much does it cost to use another bank's ATM?**

_____

Another bank's ATM is often referred to as "out of network." ATM fees generally run $3 or so per transaction.

8. **What's the point of sale fee (POS)?** _____

A POS fee is when you pay at a store with your debit card. The bank may have a fee and the merchant (store) may have a fee, too.

 WARNING: *When you pay at the pump for gas with your debit card, the gas station has the right to put a hold on the money in your account for up to three days over and above the amount you get in gas.*

 Get a copy of the bank's fee schedule and look it over to find out all of the additional fees that may nickel and dime you later. You'll be blown away by all the fees they can charge you!

9. **When do you put checks on hold and how long will the hold be?** _____

When you deposit a check in the ATM, via mobile device or at the branch, your bank may put a hold on your check until they can verify the check is good. This means the money is in the bank, but you don't have access to it yet.

10. **When and why do you report someone to ChexSystems?**

_____

A ChexSystems report generally happens when you mishandle an account or abuse an account and leave an account overdrawn for too long. Having a ChexSystems report prohibits you from opening new accounts for up to five years. You can find out if you have a record and get more information by visiting consumerdebit.com. You're entitled to a free copy of your report every 12 months.

KEEP TRACK OF YOUR TRANSACTIONS

One of the most important things you need to do with an account is keep track of your transactions and do the math. It's too dangerous to just keep a running tally in your head. So make sure you keep track by entering all of your transactions (deposits, withdrawals, ATM, debit card, checks written, and fees) in a check register, computer software, a spreadsheet, or a digital app like mint.com so you always know how much money is in your account.

SET UP ACCOUNT ALERTS

One of the easiest, most effective ways to help manage your account and avoid overdraft fees is to set up account alerts. Most banks allow you to set them up for free and they will notify you by email, text message, or phone about the activity on your account. A few important alerts to consider setting up: low balance, account overdrawn, debit card, bill payment, and ATM withdrawal.

BALANCE YOUR ACCOUNT AT LEAST MONTHLY

Balancing your account is super easy and extremely important to do so you avoid being overdrawn and getting charged excessive fees. To balance your account, all you have to do is look at your balance, add deposits you've made that are not showing up, and subtract any transactions that haven't cleared your account. The amount you come up with should be the same on your statement or that shows online.

The benefit of balancing your account each month is that if something is wrong, you can get it fixed quickly. Often you have a limited amount of time—30 to 60 days—to correct mistakes and get your money back if it's a bank error, and mistakes do happen; you and your banker are human.

WHAT TO DO IF SOMETHING GOES WRONG

 Banker's Secret

If something goes wrong with your account, an issue comes up, or you have a special request, make sure you:

Time it right. Go to the bank to deal with it when the bank isn't busy. Avoid busy days like the 1st, 3rd, 15th, and last day of the month and lunch hours. Thursdays are a great day of the week to go into a bank, specifically around 10 a.m., before lunch hours start. This when you're most likely to receive undivided attention.

Ask the right person. Any time you need something special— a hold removed, fees waived, or any type of exception, make sure you ask the right person. Everyone in the branch has approval limits. Limits go up with the position held—teller, supervisor, assistant manager, manager, regional manager, and beyond. The more serious the issue, the higher you may have to go to get what you need done.

Be nice. Above all, when you're at the bank, be nice. You get much more with honey than with vinegar. You can try saying something like this: "Can you help me? I'm so embarrassed and I'm not sure how this happened! I've always been very careful with [mention your issue]...."

Keep good records. You and the bank have a shared responsibility to make sure things are correct on your account. The bank will send you monthly statements, email alerts, text messages, and all kinds of stuff. It's your job as the customer to read the information they send. *If you find an error, it's important to correct it immediately* because you may have a limited timeframe to get things corrected or to get your money back. It's best to get serious issues documented in writing and keep the documents in your banking file (see page 106). Never rely on a bank employee remembering your situation or assume that person will always be working for the bank. It's best to get issues taken care of *in writing on bank letterhead.*

HOW TO GUARD AGAINST IDENTITY THEFT

Identity thieves are smarter than ever and are out there lurking around every corner, quietly waiting to steal your identity. They can wipe out your bank accounts, max out your credit cards, and use your identity to establish their life here in the U.S. The crooks can even use your ID when they're caught, leaving you with a criminal record or an active arrest warrant if they skip town!

If you can fill in the blanks based on what you've posted on social media sites, so can an identity thief:

All about me: I was born in the year _____ in the beautiful city of _____. My mother's maiden name is _____. Growing up, my favorite house was the one on _____ Street. We had a dog named _____. I'm now ___ years old and live in downtown _____. I'm married and our anniversary date is _____. We have ___ lovely children named _____ _____. My social security number is ___-___-_____.

☐ **Protect your Social Security number.** Don't carry your Social Security card or number with you, and use caution when sharing your Social Security number. If you are asked for your Social Security number, know why the person needs it, how he will use it, how he will protect it, and what will happen if you don't give it to him.

☐ **There are secrets in your trash.** Treat your mail and trash carefully. Never leave mail in your mailbox overnight. Shred mail with personal identifiers, especially anything with account numbers (credit card statements, bank statements, insurance forms, medical statements, receipts, pre-approved credit offers) so thieves can't pick through your trash or recycling bin and do bad things with your numbers. You can have your name removed from direct marketing lists by opting out of junk mail—go to optoutprescreen.com or call 1-888-5-OPT-OUT (1-888-567-8688).

 How to Check on Your Bank and Medical Activity

You can keep tabs on bank account activity under your name by getting your annual free copy of your consumer report at consumerdebit.com. Medical insurance activity can be obtained by writing to your insurance company and requesting an Annual Statement of Medical Benefits. Prescription drug history can be obtained by calling Intelliscript or Medpoint.

❏ **Verify sources before sharing information.** Scammers pretend to be people you know or already do business with. DON'T give out or confirm personal information through unsolicited contact. If you are contacted, look up their contact information on your own. DON'T click on links, reply to emails, respond to text messages, or engage in phone conversations.

❏ **Use strong passwords.** Never use the same password for everything or use information in a password that could be easily found. DON'T use your name, date of birth, any part of your

Social Security number, old phone numbers, anniversaries, or consecutive numbers.

☐ **Safeguard your purse and wallet.** Always keep an eye on it and only carry the identification and cards you need.

☐ **Be careful on the Internet.** Many people put way too much personal information online, and criminals can find ways to use it to their advantage. Do not answer quizzes on social media sites, do understand your privacy settings on all of your accounts, and don't browse sensitive sites on public Wi-Fi. When shopping online and checking out, always make sure you see "https://" (the "s" stands for secure); it will often appear with a lock symbol next to it. Know who you're dealing with. If you're unfamiliar with a company, research it by doing a quick Internet search. It's all too easy to click around and find yourself in a bad part of cyber town.

☐ **Watch your credit.** Annually pull your credit reports at annualcreditreport.com. Check your name, address(es), and Social Security number, and verify your current and past employers. Look for things like accounts you didn't open and inquiries from companies you can't explain.

More information on identity theft can be found at ftc.gov.

BOTTOM LINE

Bank accounts are important and help us manage our money in day-to-day life, but they shouldn't cost us a bunch of money. It's our job to be educated consumers and optimize our relationships with financial institutions.

CHAPTER SIX

Borrowing—Be a Smart Borrower

In today's society, the reality is that one day you will have to borrow money and deal with credit because it's really hard to save up $25,000 cash to buy a car or $150,000 cash to buy a house. Borrowing money can get very tricky—it's easy to get lured in over your head and it can be extremely expensive if you don't follow a few simple rules. Having debt (an outstanding loan) is like having a ball and chain around your ankle; it robs you of your freedom. Outstanding debt gives a lender a right to a portion of everything you earn until the loan is paid off.

Never borrow more than you can afford to repay.

I can't stress this enough: **Never borrow more than you can afford to repay.** You will be tempted because everywhere you turn, someone wants to sell you something. They want you to spend your hard-earned money on their product so they can make a buck. We are exposed to more than 1,500 advertisements per day…buy this…buy that. We're even pressured to feel like it's our "job" to go out and spend all of our money, or money we don't have, to stimulate the economy. Ah, but these companies have a solution for that—a loan or a credit card—and THAT is when it gets really scary. It's easy to be driven by desire.

 Don't Be This Guy!

I know a guy who graduated college with a good degree and got his first job making a whopping $85,000 per year. He felt like he had "made it," so he bought a brand spanking new Mercedes for $45,000. The car dealership happily approved him for the loan, so in his mind, he could afford it. What's really sad is that he went into the dealership asking how much of a loan he could be approved for—he didn't know his numbers before he went in. He got so excited about the new car after he took it for a test drive—he wanted it so badly, he quickly forgot about his rent, student loans, how much the insurance would cost, or what the gas mileage would be.

Buying the car turned out to be a very expensive decision: that decision cost him $20,250! Three years later when the newness wore off and he realized his car was costing him a small fortune, he went to sell the car and found out it had dropped in value. His $45,000 car was now only worth $24,750—that's $20,250 less than when he bought it! In all, it was an expensive move to buy that new car because new cars depreciate (lose value) 40% within the first three years. This car had also cost him dearly in even more ways: on expensive insurance premiums because it was the luxury sport model, on gas because it got bad gas mileage, and on the annual state registration, which was costly. How long will he have to work to recover the many thousands of dollars he lost on that car?

THINK LIKE A BANKER

Here's how borrowing money works.

Any time you borrow money, it's going to cost you: The bank/ lender will charge you interest. The amount of interest is based on your ability to repay the loan (do you have a job and how long have you had it?) and what your reputation is for paying your bills on time and in full in the past (your credit history). They will also look at what you're borrowing money to buy: Is it something they can take back ("collateral") and sell if you don't make your payments, like a car (think repo man), or is it something they can't get back, like clothes, food, or drink ("unsecured")? It's called "risk-based pricing"—they evaluate how much risk is profitable to them and price loans accordingly.

> SPECIAL NOTE: The next chapter on credit scores and your credit history is SUPER important—it's what could cost you or save you thousands, if not hundreds of thousands, of dollars over your lifetime. You HAVE to read it; it's a game changer.

FOUR QUESTIONS TO ASK YOURSELF BEFORE YOU BORROW MONEY

1. **Why** _____ ?

   Why you are borrowing money? Is it for something that will make you money? Will it increase or decrease in value? Is to provide enjoyment or is it a necessity? You can also go into debt for unexpected reasons: an accident, illness, job loss, divorce, death, poor planning, or simply ignorance, greed, or not paying attention to your financial situation because you're overwhelmed.

   WARNING: *Watch what you charge on your credit card—the interest can be very expensive! A good rule of thumb to follow is to never charge anything that you eat, drink, or wear. If you do, it's very easy to charge more than you can afford to pay off each month, resulting in very expensive pizza, beer, or jeans down the road. A $2,000 credit card balance at 29% interest costs roughly $50 a month, $600 a year. How many hours will you have to work just to pay the interest? Is that money you're willing to walk away from to have that immediate gratification?*

2. **Can I afford it?**   Yes _____ No _____

   This will look familiar because I talked about it in chapter 4 on budgeting, but it's so important that I'm going to repeat the information here.

Review your budget carefully every time you consider borrowing money. You need to know what you can truly afford. Be honest with yourself.

 Banker's Secret

It's unfortunate, but many lenders will approve you for much more of a loan than you can actually afford! Remember that the lender and the loan officer make money off of each loan they fund, and sometimes that means *your* best interest isn't their top priority. *This is why it's imperative* that YOU know your own numbers and YOU tell the lender what you can afford, not the other way around.

 To be safe, "live as if" for three months with your new payment to make sure you can really afford it. Living as if means paying yourself the difference between your current payment and the new one you're considering. It's also extremely important to include any additional expenses your new payment will incur. A new car might have more expensive registration and insurance or get different gas mileage. A new home might have more expensive utilities, yard care, and maintenance, or you could experience higher transportation costs to work/school from your new home location.

Bankers/lenders use something called your *debt-to-income ratio* to calculate how much of a loan you should be able to afford.

It's Your Money

As I mentioned in chapter 4, new guidelines established in 2014 will allow you to borrow up to 43% of your gross income—but a safer number to use (which I highly recommend) is the previous standard conventional loan debt-to-income ratios, which are 28/36. This means no more than 28% of your gross income should be spent on housing (rent/lease/mortgage payment, insurance, and taxes), and no more than 36% of your gross income should be spent on housing PLUS recurring debt (auto loans, credit cards, student loans, child support, alimony, etc.).

Now let's run your numbers the same way to figure out what payment you can afford:

Yearly gross income* = _____ / divided by 12
= _____ monthly income

Monthly gross income _____ x 0.28
= _____ allotted for housing expense

Monthly gross income _____ x 0.36
= _____ allotted for housing expense plus all recurring debt

− _____ existing housing expense
− _____ existing recurring debt
= _____ new payment you can afford

*Gross income = income before tax and other deductions are taken out of your income

Here's an example:

Yearly gross income = __$45,000__ / divided by 12
= __$3,750__ monthly income

Monthly gross income __$3,750__ x 0.28
= __$1,050__ allotted for housing expense

Monthly income __$3,750__ x 0.36
= __$1,350__ allotted for housing expense plus all recurring debt

– $1,050 existing housing expense (rent)
– $200 existing recurring debt (car and credit card payment)
= $100 new payment you can afford

---

3. **What's my credit score right now?** _____
   (See chapter 7 on credit.)

4. **Who has the best deal?** _____
   Shop the competition before you apply, because each time you apply for a loan, it can bring down your credit score.

FIVE QUESTIONS TO ASK WHEN SHOPPING FOR A CREDIT CARD

1. **Annual percentage rates (APRs)**
   Introductory APR: _____
   Purchase APR: _____
   Balance transfer APR: _____
   Cash advance APR: _____
   Penalty APR: _____

2. **Fees**
   Annual fee: _____
   Late payment fee: _____
   Phone payment fee: _____
   Over-limit fee: _____
   Returned item fee: _____
   Balance transfer fee: _____
   Convenience check fee: _____
   Cash advance fee: _____
   Foreign transfer fee: _____

3. **Due date**
   When are payments due? _____

   Generally, you have 21 full days to make a payment after your bill has been mailed or delivered. Your payment should also be due on the same date each month.

4. Grace period

Is there a grace period, and if so, how long is it? _____

Some cards will not charge you interest on purchases if you pay your entire balance by the due date each month. If they offer a grace period, you can avoid paying interest during that period.

5. Rewards

How are rewards earned? _____

What kind of rewards can be earned? _____

How can rewards be spent? _____

 Credit cards are heavily marketed and convenient to use. They have become a way of life for many people. It's easy to say to yourself "I can pay this off at the end of the month" when you make the charge.

To avoid getting sucked into that trap, try this if you frequently use credit cards. When you charge a credit card, write each charge in your check register in red ink just like it was a debit or ATM withdrawal. That way, at the end of the month, if you have done all of your accounting correctly, you will have enough to pay the credit card balance in full, avoiding expensive interest and going into debt.

THIRTEEN QUESTIONS TO ASK WHEN SHOPPING FOR LOANS (AUTO, HOME, ETC.)

1. What is the rate? _____

2. What is the annual percentage rate (APR)? _____

   WARNING: *APR = fees expressed as a rate. If there is a difference between the rate and APR, there are fees for the loan.*

3. Is the rate fixed or variable? _____
   Fixed means the rate will not change for the entire term of the loan or a set period.

   If the rate is *variable,* ask these questions:

   What index is it tied to? _____
   How often can my rate change? _____
   How much can it change? _____

   WARNING: *If you have a variable interest rate negative amortization loan, your payment could change (and go up) and so could your balance. So ask and understand when and how this could happen.*

4. What is the loan amount? _____

5. What is my monthly payment? _____

6. Will the monthly payment always be the same or can it change? _____

7. What is the term/number of payments? _____

8. When is the payment due? _____

9. When is my payment considered "late" and what is the late fee? _____

10. What is the finance charge? _____
The finance charge is the total dollar amount the loan will cost you over the life of the loan.

11. What is the prepayment penalty? _____

12. Is there a balloon payment? _____

   WARNING: *If you have a balloon payment, it's critical that you know when it's due and how it can be handled.*

13. Can the loan be assumed? _____
"Assumed" means having someone take over your existing loan terms.

BONUS QUESTION: WHAT WOULD THE INTEREST RATE AND PAYMENT BE FOR DIFFERENT TERMS?

Here's why you want to ask this bonus question: Shorter terms generally mean lower interest rates, and lower interest rates can mean huge savings!

Loan amount $300,000	15-year mortgage 3.39%	30-year mortgage 4.27%
Monthly payment	$2,128.48	$1,479.33
Difference between the two payments	$649.15	
Total payments	$2,128.48 x 12 months x 15 years = $383,126.40	$1,479.33 x 12 months x 30 years = $532,588.80
Total interest	$83,126.17	$232,588.80

Interest Rate Source bankrate.com, 8/20/14

In this scenario, the difference between the payment for the 15-year loan and the 30-year loan is $649.15 a month. Opting for the 15-year mortgage would save you $149,462.63 in interest over the life of the loan…now that's BIG money!

This is one of the best money power plays I've ever made. When I was 18, I bought my first house, and thank goodness I asked the bonus question! The difference between a 15-year payment and a 30-year payment at the time wasn't much at all, and I happily opted for the 15-year higher payment, vowing to figure out a way to suck it up and find a way to make the higher payment so I wouldn't have to make mortgage payments for an additional 15 years.

ONCE APPROVED, WHAT TO CHECK BEFORE YOU SIGN ON THE DOTTED LINE

Read the fine print! Know what it says in the documents you're signing. Don't take the banker's word for anything; *you have to verify it for yourself.* Bankers are human and they can make mistakes. I was one of them—and here's what happened to me and one of my customers.

At the bank where I worked, I had been signing hundreds of home equity loans and lines of credit for my clients, allowing them access to the equity in their home to spend as they wished. One day when I was out sick, the bank changed the rules of the loan. To inform the bankers of the change, the bank sent a 25-page email with a teeny-tiny, itsy-bitsy section about a new prepayment penalty.

When I came back the next day, I sat down with a customer before I read my email, and as we were signing his loan documents, I asked him if he wanted to read the documents or if he wanted me to give him the nutshell version. He asked for the short version, and I told him there was no prepayment penalty—he could pay this off and close it at any time at no cost.

What I didn't realize is that the previous day, in that 25-page email, things had changed—and now there *was* a prepayment penalty!

It was an honest mistake. I didn't purposely misguide my customer. I am human, and I had missed the new, important information in that long email. Missing this one important bit of prepayment information cost this man $6,000 two years later when he sold his house. From that day on, I always said to customers who were signing a loan: "It is my current understanding that there is no prepayment penalty; however, please read it yourself."

So don't just take your banker's word, and remember that any time you get a loan product from a bank, the person you're dealing with will most likely make a commission—and on top of that commission, the bank is going to make money.

You have to be an educated consumer, read the fine print, and ask questions whenever you're evaluating a loan or signing documents to obtain a loan.

HOW TO READ LOAN DOCUMENTS

When you sign loan documents, they will have bullet points. Read and make sure you understand them. You can use the previous loan checklists to confirm that the loan you applied for is the same loan you're signing for. If you have questions, ask now. Once you sign and you receive the funds, there's no going back saying you didn't understand. You signed for the loan, you got the money—now you have to pay.

SIX STEPS TO GET OUT OF DEBT

We've established that we can get into debt for all kinds of reasons, and it's easy to get in over our heads and become overwhelmed. Remember that financial stress affects almost every aspect of our lives—relationships, health, productivity at work, and self-esteem.

If you ever find yourself in over your head with too much debt, the first thing you want to do is STOP! Just like if you were lost in the forest, stop and spend some time figuring out where you are and come up with some strategies to get yourself out of the situation.

Step 1: Immediately stop charging your credit cards and obtaining new loans.

Step 2: Put all of your credit cards in an envelope (cut them up if you think you can't trust yourself) and write on the outside of the envelope all of the bad things that being in debt has caused you. This way, if you're ever tempted to go into debt again or if you reach for your cards, you'll be reminded in your own words why you don't want to let this happen again.

Step 3: Get your credit card statements and chart out how much you owe, to whom, what your payments are, when they're due, what the interest rate is, and how much the monthly finance charge is. Seeing all of this—especially how much being in debt is costing you in finance charges each month—will motivate you further. (See "Get Out of Debt Priority Worksheet Sample," on page 76.)

Step 4: Prioritize your accounts to be paid off in one of following ways. Each one works and will get your debt paid off in the most effective and efficient order for you. Pick the one you like best.

❒ **Pay the highest interest rate first.** Mathematically this makes the most sense because you're getting rid of the most expensive debt first. However, that may take a long time if you have a high balance—you might lose interest or get discouraged and give up.

❒ **Pay the lowest balance first.** Known as the "Debt Snowball" method, this strategy was popularized by Dave Ramsey. Emotionally, this one may feel the best. When you pay off a small debt and quickly get to move to the next slightly larger target, you can quickly build momentum and see your success—which will motivate you to keep on plowing down your debt.

❒ **Pay the least number of payments left/due first.** Logically this works well, too, but it isn't as popular because it takes a bit more work. However, it can be an extremely effective option. You can figure out how many payments you have left on installment loans (loans with a fixed interest rate, loan amount, and term, like cars) by looking at your statement or by dividing your balance by the monthly payment amount. For credit cards, you'll need to go to a site like bankrate.com and use the credit card payoff calculator. David Bach made this option popular with his Debt Free for Life book; he calls it the DOLP Method®.

How intensely do you feel about the debt?

Figuring this out can be liberating and start you toward recovery. During one of my corporate workshops, a woman broke down in tears when we came to this question—she had never thought about how debt from her divorce represented one of the hardest times in her life and some of the most ridiculous spending choices she had ever made. She never considered how much her debt was affecting her self-esteem and how much it had been weighing her down. Once she decided on a get-out-of-debt strategy and set it in motion, she felt empowered, unstoppable, and on the road to being healed.

GET OUT OF DEBT PRIORITY WORKSHEET SAMPLE

Account	Interest Rate	Balance	Monthly Minimum Payment	Monthly Finance Charge (This is how much it's costing you in interest each month)	# of Payments Left	Payment Due Date
Master Card	29.9%	$2,000	$100	$49.15	28 Use a credit card payoff calculator on the Internet	15th of the month
Auto Loan	5.50%	$5,500	$250	$24.41	22 Check your statement, use a payoff calculator on the Internet, or divide your balance by your monthly payment	1st of the month

Remember all debt: Credit cards, student loans, auto, recreational vehicle, family, friends, medical, dental, vision, veterinary bills, debt consolidation, personal loans, bank overdraft, department store, collections, back child support, back taxes, home equity loans and lines, mortgages, second homes, vacation or timeshare, furniture, computers, appliances, or whatever.

GET OUT OF DEBT PRIORITY WORKSHEET

Account	Interest Rate	Balance	Monthly Minimum Payment	Monthly Finance Charge (This is how much it's costing you in interest each month)	# of Payments Left	Payment Due Date

Step 5: Start paying down your debt. Each month, as the payments are due, make the minimum payment on every account except the one you've identified as your primary priority target. For your first targeted debt, make your minimum payment PLUS anything and everything you can over the minimum payment amount. Shoot for two to three times the minimum payment due.

Step 6: Once you've paid off your target debt, move to the next one and do the same thing.

HOW TO GET OUT OF DEBT FASTER

There are several things you can do:

❏ Strategically use windfalls like your tax return, bonuses, overtime, holiday gifts, etc.

❏ Look around your house and see if you have any items you can sell at a yard sale or on the Internet, especially if you have a storage unit (no need to pay to store stuff you're not using). You'd be amazed at how much money you can come up with. A few months ago, some of my friends had a yard sale and sold more than $700 of stuff! That money could be used to pay down debt.

❏ See if you have any recycling you can cash in—cans, bottles, aluminum, or copper. You might have enough to turn what some consider trash into cash.

❏ Sell really nice items at consignment stores. A variety of stores will take furniture, clothing, electronics, etc. They take a commission from what's sold and give you the rest. Some will even pay for it on the spot.

❏ Cut your spending and live on 10% less. You can find out how to reduce your monthly bills on sites like billshrink.com.

❏ Use coupons as an additional source of cash (coupons just look like paper, but they are really money).

HOW TO GET HELP

If you ever find yourself in trouble and in over your head, there are resources out there for you. A great place to start is The National Foundation for Credit Counseling (nfcc.org) or another nonprofit consumer-credit counseling service.

BOTTOM LINE

Borrowing money is a reality for most of us and we have to be smart about it. We have to ask questions—both of ourselves and the person lending us the money—and be sure we understand the answers. When we sign on the dotted line and accept someone's else's money in the form of a loan, it gives them a right to a portion of our paycheck. It's like a ball and chain attached to us until that loan is paid off.

CHAPTER SEVEN

Credit—Know the Critical Ins and Outs of Credit

WHAT YOUR CREDIT CONSISTS OF

Your credit consists of two things: your *credit report* (also known as your *credit history*) and your *credit score.* Together, they play a critical role in your financial life. They are used for much more than just borrowing money from the bank.

WHO'S LOOKING AT YOUR CREDIT AND HOW THEY'RE USING IT

❐ **Banks and lenders** use your credit score to determine your credit risk, and that influences whether they should approve or deny your loan request, and how much of an interest rate they should charge you.

❐ **Employers** sometimes look at your credit profile to see if they should hire you because they know people with bad credit can be financially stressed out. If you're financially stressed out, you might be fighting with your spouse, which means you could be distracted at work. Employers also know that if you're stressed out, your immune system will be suppressed, so you'll probably miss more days of work or be tardy. And they figure that if you have bad credit, you might even be tempted to steal because you're in a desperate situation.

❏ **Landlords** look at credit scores to find out whether or not you're going to pay your rent on time, which will determine whether they'll rent to you.

❏ **Many auto and home insurance companies** use your credit to determine whether to insure you and how much your premiums should cost.

❏ **Cell phone companies** look at credit scores to find out whether or not you should have a cell phone plan with them—they want to make sure you'll be able to pay.

HOW MUCH HAVING BAD CREDIT COSTS

Having bad credit can literally *cost you thousands—if not hundred of thousands—of dollars over your lifetime.*

Here's an example. Before my husband and I got married, I checked his credit (he pulled his reports and I looked over them with an eagle eye; it was an "I'll show you mine if you show me yours" kind of deal we made with each other) because I wanted to see what I was getting myself into. I knew how his credit score could impact our quality of life together—if he could get a job, if we could rent an apartment, buy a car, get insurance for the car, and stuff like that. When I checked it, I found out that he had a $40 collection from a pager dispute that he wasn't going to pay based on the principle of the matter, and I was fine with that. But here's what happened: That $40 collection cost us $15,000! Here's how. When we went to buy our house and get a mortgage loan, his credit score had dropped a tiny bit to 719, which made us miss a loan discount of 0.25% for people with good credit. So that $40 collection actually cost us $15,000 in extra interest! Not cool.

WHAT A CREDIT REPORT IS

A credit report contains the all of the details about any loan you currently have or have had in the past. When you borrow money from a lender, the lender reports all of your activity—what types of credit you use, when the account was opened, how much you borrowed, what the balance is, and if you've made your payments on time to one of three major credit reporting bureaus: TransUnion, Equifax, and Experian. These three agencies do not share information between them; they each run independent companies that collect, store, and furnish information about your credit history. Where it gets tricky is the fact that lenders are not required to—and often do not—report your information to all three credit bureaus, so the information on each one of your reports is most likely going to be different.

KNOW YOUR CREDIT BUREAU RIGHTS

Each year you are entitled to a free copy of your credit report from each bureau. Staying on top of your credit history is critical for several reasons. Research shows that at any given time, roughly 80% of Americans have an error on their credit report, and 25% of those errors are so serious that they would cause you to be denied for a loan. Getting a copy of your credit report every 12 months also helps you make sure someone hasn't stolen your identity. You can get your free copies from annualcreditreport.com. Your credit *reports* are free, but if you want your credit *score*, you'll have to pay for it—the cost is about $10. Be aware that the score they provide may not be the same as what lenders use.

 WARNING: *Resist the ads for credit monitoring services! Credit monitoring offers limited protection and can be pricey. You can stay on top of your own credit for free, get your own free reports each year, and keep a close eye on your credit card statements and bank account activity.*

HOW TO GET YOUR FREE REPORTS

Before you visit **annualcreditreport.com**, here are three tips:

1. Make sure you have a few minutes, because if you get interrupted or time out, it can be difficult to pick up where you left off.
2. Make sure you have a full paper tray. You'll want to pull each of your reports and print them out so you can read them very carefully.
3. Have an extra ink cartridge on hand in case you run out of ink.

*Be sure to download or print out **all three reports**—one from Trans-Union, one from Equifax, and one from Experian—because the information on each report will most likely be different.*

 If you want to save paper and ink, you can download the reports as PDFs, view them on your computer screen, and make notes from there.

WHAT TO DO WITH YOUR CREDIT REPORTS

1. **Look for errors.** Once you've printed out all three reports, go over them with a fine-toothed comb. Look for accounts that you've opened and make sure everything is accurate—credit limit, balance, payment history, etc. Look for accounts that have been paid off but still show up as open, and old information that should have been removed (most of the time it's seven years until it's removed, with the exception of Chapter 7 bankruptcy, which stays on for 10 years).

 Banker's Secret

Under credit inquiries, you will see two different types. The first type—inquiries made by you (applying for something, when you signed and authorized the credit check)—do count against your credit score. The second type—inquiries made by companies you already have credit with—do not count against your score. They're like a nosy neighbor peeking over the fence, seeing what you're doing with all of your other credit accounts. They use what they see to make decisions about your existing and future credit accounts with them—whether to increase, decrease, or even close your credit line.

---

2. **Detect identity theft.** Make sure you check your name, address(es), and Social Security number, and verify your current and past employers. Look for things like accounts you didn't open and inquiries from companies you can't explain. (See identity theft section in chapter 5 on banking.)

3. **Dispute incorrect information.** If you find an error, you must make the effort to get it fixed NOW, not later. It may take some work, but it will be worth your while, since so much is riding on your credit profile (jobs, interest rates, insurance rates, etc.). It's your right to dispute incorrect information, and the credit bureaus must respond and investigate on your behalf.

WHAT A CREDIT SCORE IS

Your credit score is commonly referred to as your *FICO score* (FICO stands for Fair Isaac Corporation, a Minneapolis company whose scores are used in an estimated 90% of U.S. credit decisions). It's a three-digit number ranging from 300 to 850; higher is better. Your credit score is used by lenders to determine your creditworthiness. Since there are three different credit reporting agencies—TransUnion, Equifax, and Experian—and information on each one of those reports will most likely be different, it means you will have three different credit scores just like you have three different credit reports.

FYI: *Other scores exist, like the VantageScore and TransRisk score, but lenders rarely use them to make credit-based decisions.*

HOW CREDIT SCORES ARE CALCULATED

Your credit score is calculated by pulling information from one of your credit reports through a statistical five-point matrix assessment, and each point of that matrix has a different level of importance.

Here's the breakdown:

    35% - payment history
    30% - amounts owed
    15% - length of credit history
    10% - new credit
    10% - types of credit used

Your credit score, or FICO score, does not include factors such as age, nation of origin, gender, religion, educational level, or marital status. It's important to remember that your credit score is just like a picture—it's a financial snapshot of a specific point in time. It captures several different elements and changes as things change: when you make payments, when you charge on your credit card, or when you get new loans.

It's important to remember that your credit score is like a snapshot, like taking a picture of your current credit activity. Activity from the past will fade away and your current activity will eventually replace it. To achieve and keep a good score, you have to demonstrate your ability to be consistently responsible.

HOW TO ESTABLISH CREDIT

If you're new to the credit game, you'll have to apply for a lot of different credit cards and types of loans before somebody will finally trust you with your first loan or credit card. Once you get that first loan, you have to prove that you're worthy of having it by making your payments on time. If you do well and make all of your payments on time with small amounts of someone's money, they will eventually trust you with larger amounts of their money. If you're irresponsible and don't make your payments on time, they will think twice about loaning you more money, and if they do decide to give you a loan, they know it's riskier and will charge you dearly in the way of higher interest rates. It costs a lot for them to collect from you—they have to send you notices, call you, and try to collect their money—and they will make sure they're paid for their time and money.

It's important to start establishing credit early in life because it takes time to build and establish a good credit history. It's like climbing a ladder—it takes time and effort. You have to be stable on the first step and earn the right to advance and take the next step. Here's a typical example:

CLIMBING THE CREDIT LADDER

$500 (your first credit card)

$1,500 (12 months later, they increase your credit limit)

$3,000 (18 months later, they increase your credit limit again)

$7,000 (6 months later, it's time to buy a new car)

$15,000 (6 months later, that car breaks down; you need a better car)

$25,000 (you've met and married your soulmate, you're having a baby, you need a van)

$100,000 (2 years later, you have another baby, the housing market is good, it's time to buy a house)

If you were late on the $500 credit card, would they increase your credit limit to $2,500? Nope. And if you were late on the $7,000 car loan, would they lend you $15,000? I think not.

If you were a banker and I walked into the bank with NO credit history at all, would you lend me $100,000 not knowing if I can make the payments on smaller amounts on time? Probably not! I'll bet you would want to see my credit history in order to make your decision. I know it sounds crazy, but no credit is not good credit in this case.

HOW TO IMPROVE YOUR SCORE

The general rule is the more recent and consistent your activity is, whether it's good or bad, the bigger impact it has on your score. You can't get negative accurate information removed from your credit report, so don't fall for "credit repair" scams out there that say they can do it. You can, however, start improving your credit score, starting today.

☐ **Make your payments on time.** If you have accounts past due, get them current, and stay current on all of your debts. Remember, 35% (the biggest factor) of your score is based on your payment history.

☐ **Keep your balances low or paid off.** One of the quickest ways to improve your score is to pay down and keep balances on your credit cards low or paid off. Only use a small portion (30% or less) of your available credit lines. Thirty percent of your score is based on how much you owe.

 WARNING: *Lenders can increase, decrease, or cancel any credit card at any time for any reason (you will find this type of verbiage in the fine print of your agreement with them). So don't get addicted to your credit...because it's THEIR money!*

☐ **Don't close unused or paid-off credit cards.** If you do, it may lower your score because it shrinks your available credit limit. Remember that 30% of your score is based on the amounts you owe versus your available credit.

❒ **Limit applying for credit.** Only apply to open new accounts when you *need* to, not just when you want to.

 *If you're having trouble getting approved for your first credit card or are trying to reestablish your credit, a secured credit card might work for you. A secured credit card is when a lender requires you to deposit a certain amount of your own money in an account and gives you a credit line against it. They will most likely charge you an annual fee and the card will have a fairly high interest rate. Make sure you look specifically for **secured** credit cards, not **prepaid** credit cards. Secured credit cards generally report to the three major credit bureaus, your money is refundable when the line is closed, and you may eventually qualify for an unsecured card. You can use a secured credit card like any major credit card. You can compare cards on sites like* **creditcards.org** *or* **creditcards.com***.*

CREDIT HORROR STORIES

❒ **Don't co-sign on a loan:** As a banker, I had a customer who owned a motorcycle shop. One day he came into the bank and was super excited because he had just sold a motorcycle. He said that three weeks earlier, a guy wanted to buy a motorcycle, but had bad credit. He asked the guy if he had a girlfriend. The guy said no. The shop owner said that when the guy got a girlfriend, if she had good credit, he could bring her in and see if she'd co-sign on the loan so he could get the bike. Well, guess what? The guy had come back into the shop with his new girlfriend, and she co-signed the loan so he could get the bike. How long do you think the guy and girl were together? Not long! They broke up, and the guy kept the bike and stuck her with the payments because he didn't make them—which ruined *her* credit. So NEVER co-sign on a loan with anybody. If you do, you are obligated to pay that money back—whether you like the person or not.

❏ **Repo man:** When I was a bank manager, I had an employee who was a college student and lived about 30 miles away. She had a car and would drive to work each day. She always had her school-books, camera, music, and a change of clothes with her, so when she came to town, she'd go to work and then go straight to school or out partying. She started getting a lot of phone calls at work from a collection company that was trying to get her to make her car payments, and she was really stressed out. One day I looked outside and there was a tow truck towing her car away—her car got repossessed. She was devastated. She could no longer get to work or school or go out with her friends without having to bum a ride or take the bus. She lost a lot of her freedom when she stopped making her car payments. Make your payments!

❏ **Bad credit = no job:** I knew a guy who had been training and going to school for a special job. He came to find out during the hiring process that the company he wanted to work for did a background check that included checking his credit. Unfortunately, his bad credit took him out of the job candidate pool, so he wasn't able to get the job that he had trained so hard for and went to school for.

BOTTOM LINE

When you add up the higher interest rates, insurance bills, and lost job opportunities, your credit score could literally cost you— or save you—hundreds of thousands of dollars over your lifetime. So only apply for credit when you need it, always make your payments, and check your three credit reports once a year to be sure everything looks okay.

BOTTOM LINE

CHAPTER EIGHT

Organization—Organize Your Finances

THE BENEFITS OF BEING ORGANIZED

Being financially organized is a great way to make the most of your financial situation, reduce stress, and build your confidence.

Here are just a few examples of why being organized is important:

❏ Have you ever missed a payment, been charged a late fee, and taken a hit on your credit score because a bill got buried under piles of paper or was accidently thrown away?

❏ Have you ever tossed a receipt into the trash, only later to wish you had it because you needed to return an item—and now you've lost out on that money?

❏ Have you ever spent 30 minutes or an hour looking for something and had to buy a replacement?

❐ If you were selling your car, would you get more for it if you had all of the car's maintenance records—regularly scheduled service, oil changes, repairs, and other paperwork that showed you took care of the car? (I'll bet you'd get a *lot* more money for it than someone selling a car without any of that important paperwork!)

I was talking with a girlfriend about all of the benefits of financial organization, and we started discussing her particular situation. She had just bought a new place and was having trouble keeping up with all of her bills and getting organized. She had been late on a few bills and got late charges, which cost her money, and she took a hit on her credit score, too. She said she often felt overwhelmed with all of the pressure, and sometimes she got sick of looking at the stacks of mail and paperwork, so she just tossed some of it.

> **Financial organization is the foundation of a solid financial life.**

I offered to help her get organized, and what I found when I arrived at her home was pretty typical—maybe you can relate to this. She took me around her house, showing me where she kept her mail, paid her bills, and filed important paperwork. She led me to her kitchen, where there was a pile of mail and other papers. She took me to her guest room, where there was a desk with more stacks of unopened mail and miscellaneous paperwork. I noticed a shredder in the corner covered with more papers and receipts. I looked around and noticed a few shopping bags with more mail and papers, so I asked about the bags. Her place is cute, decorated very nicely, and she says she keeps it that way with quick cleanups; when she has company over, she zips around the house with a shopping bag and collects all of the piles of mail and paperwork with intentions of taking care of it later. And you know what happens then…she never gets around to it.

So we collected everything and started making piles on the kitchen table: one pile for mail, one for receipts, one for car paperwork, one for house paperwork, one for coupons, and one for gift cards (we found more than $70 in unused gift cards in all of that paperwork!).

Later, we took one afternoon and set up an organization system that she would actually use, and she loved it! She said it did way more for her than she ever thought being financially organized could do—and it will for you, too!

RECEIPTS

Let's start with those pesky little pieces of paper: receipts. Most people think they're trash, but they're not! They are *cash,* lots of cash.

Here's an example of what I mean. I love Maui Jim sunglasses and pay dearly for them, but to me, they're worth it. I once paid $299 for a pair of new Maui Jim shield sunglasses and kept the receipt. I went on vacation and I dropped them and they broke—they split just over the nosepiece. This is where buying from a good company and saving your receipt pays off. When I got home, I checked out their website for warranty and repair policies, and I sent in what they requested, which included a copy of my receipt and an $11 processing fee. Within a week I had a like-new pair of sunglasses! This wouldn't have happened if I hadn't kept my receipt...and this is just one example. So we're not talking about pinching pennies here—we're talking about pinching dollars, hundreds of dollars.

Keeping receipts will allow you to take advantage of return policies, warranties, protection programs, replacement programs, and much more.

Email receipts: More and more stores are starting to offer email digital receipts *after* in-store purchases. The trouble with opting for *only* the email receipt is that you have no way to check the receipt for accuracy before leaving the store, you may not be clear about the return policy (usually noted on receipts), and you may not be as likely to participate in email and phone surveys that offer future discounts.

For now, it's best to get both email and paper receipts. As technology gets even better, more stores may start including email receipts with links to online product manuals, instructional videos, and more.

How to manage email receipts (pick one):

❐ Create a special email address specifically for email receipts. Once a retailer has your email address, they will very likely start sending you frequent emails about sales, special events, and all kinds of stuff. You don't want to be tempted to click on links and buy more stuff you don't need—so promptly opt out. Look for the word "unsubscribe," then follow the prompts.

❐ Create a special email folder for receipts and confirmations. If you don't want to create a special email address, you can always create a special folder under your regular email account.

Digital receipts: This means scanning or snapping a picture of a receipt. New cell phone apps become available all the time, and several software companies are working hard to help us manage receipts. The IRS allows digital receipts for tax filing purposes, but some stores won't allow them for return purposes. If you go this route, just make sure you know which stores will accept them.

Paper receipts: These will still be around for a really long time because moving to electronic receipts will happen gradually, and not every mom-and-pop store or retailer will offer them.

ORGANIZING YOUR RECEIPTS

WHAT YOU'LL NEED:

All you'll need to manage your receipts is an envelope. So grab any envelope—just make sure it's the right size for wherever you decide to keep it.

Carry this envelope in a place you'll actually use it, like your purse, backpack, or glove compartment of your car. There's no need for the envelope to be fancy (although the nicer it is, the more likely you might be to use it). I started with a letter-size envelope made of paper, but it got tattered and torn, so I started decorating it and covered it with scotch tape. I currently use the plastic envelopes with a closure; you can even find designer ones now. Over time, you'll find what works for you and develop a successful system naturally.

HOW TO USE IT:

After any purchase, immediately put all receipts in the envelope.

Later, transfer each receipt to its proper place for future use or future shredding. You get to decide how and when you want to sort, keep, or shred your receipts. You can choose to transfer all receipts from your envelope into a general folder and sort them once a month, quarter, or year (like I do), or sort them as you go.

Don't beat yourself up if you don't sort the receipts right away; at least you have them, and you can always organize them later.

I transfer the receipts from my purse to a folder I have in the kitchen where I put my purse, then sort them into the proper files when I have time.

Receipts for general purchases should be kept for 90 days (the time that general warranty, exchange, refund, and replacement programs usually allow). This includes clothes, household items, software, games, cleaning supplies, paper goods, etc.

Receipts for larger expenses or long-term items may be kept longer than 90 days or indefinitely. (You may even consider copying the receipt, as receipts can fade over time.)

RECEIPT FILING IDEAS

❑ **Create a filing system:** You can use a combination of materials to file your receipts—envelopes, file folders, hanging folders, plastic bags, etc.

❑ **Personal receipts:** Make a file for personal receipts like your cell phone, music player, sunglasses, jewelry, bicycle, etc.

❑ **Gift receipts:** Around the holidays this really comes in handy. Designate a special envelope and file folder for all of your holiday purchase receipts. Consider keeping these receipts for 30 to 90 days after the holiday, or longer if you start shopping earlier and ask for a gift receipt. While you're at it, ask if the store has complimentary gift-wrapping or gift boxes; believe it or not, some still do.

❒ **Electronic receipts and warranties:** Tape or affix the receipt to your purchase or place the receipt inside the warranty booklet. Then place the booklet in a plastic bag and hang it in the garage with a thumbtack, put it in the cupboard (preferably not in the junk drawer), or store the booklet in a file you create for all your warranty items.

 You want to be able to easily find this information if needed; otherwise, you may not be as willing to try using the return or warranty policy. You want to avoid thinking, "Oh, it's too much trouble to return or exchange it…I'll just throw the product away and buy another one"—which is the same as throwing your money away.

BILLS AND PAPERWORK

Use technology to help you get partially financially organized.

❒ **Set up automatic payments.** Automatic payments are great because businesses will automatically withdraw a payment each month directly from your checking account without you having to do anything except set it up and make sure you have enough money in your account. This can help you avoid late payments, free up your time because you don't even have to write a check, and save you the cost of a postage stamp.

❒ **Set up electronic statements.** Many companies will allow you to opt for paperless statements. This can be a bit risky because you have to pay close attention to your email, and it's easy to miss important information when you're tempted to delete statements without reading the fine print. (I set up automatic payments and still get paper statements, open them, read them, then put them in a "paid bills" basket.)

❑ **Set up email and text alerts.** Many companies will allow you to set up email and text alerts for things like payment due, payment received, balance at a certain amount, and other reminders. This can be extremely helpful.

SETTING UP A FINANCIAL ORGANIZATION SYSTEM

Setting up a financial organization system and maintaining it doesn't have to be a massive undertaking. If you're just starting out, that's perfect—no backtracking for you. If you're already dealing with money, no worries—just set up your system and start using it ASAP. Then if you have time and want to go back and get what you've already organized and put it into the new system, cool; if not, it's not the end of the world. The goal here is to establish the system and start using it.

WHERE TO SET IT UP

Create a mail station where you conveniently have items that will keep you financially organized. If you want to see what this looks like, go to moneystartshere.com/financialorganization to watch a video on setting up a system. This mail station can be set up in a very small space, and it's helpful to establish the system in a convenient location in your home wherever you open your mail or pay your bills. When I was going through my divorce, I lived in a small apartment and didn't have much room, so I made a portable system by using a milk crate and hanging file folders from an office supply store, and stored it in the pantry in the kitchen. Nothing fancy, but it worked.

WHAT YOU'LL NEED

☐ A bill caddy: A place to put your bills due each month. I like to write the due date on the outside of the envelope and place the bills in date order. That way I can easily see what's due when.

☐ Envelope opener

☐ Pens

☐ Scissors

☐ Recycle bin (the perfect place to put non-sensitive junk mail)

☐ A basket or container that can hold paid bills: As technology advances, this becomes less of a big deal because of online statements. However, I'm still a big fan of getting the actual bill in the mail. I look over the document so I don't miss anything, then I pay the bill online or note the amount that will be debited for an automatic payment. I also like my paid bill basket to be decorative, so it blends in with my home office. (Yes, it's kind of "girly," but it makes me like it and want to use it.) Each January, I bundle up the previous year's paid bills and put them in the closet, and shred the year before that. I save a year's worth because I've had WAY too many times when I needed to reference paid bills, and sometimes online statements are only available for three to six months.

❒ 15 to 25 hanging file folders

❒ 15 to 25 file folders (you can use a variety of colors or decorated files for color coding and easy recognition; these will go inside the hanging file folders)

❒ Envelopes

❒ Some type of organizational box or filing cabinet

❒ A shredder

 WARNING: *Use your shredder! It's especially important to shred sensitive information. I already talked about this in the identity theft section in chapter 5 on banking, but it's an important reminder. Thieves would love to get their hands on any mail with an account number on it—from your bank, credit card company, school, insurance company, and much more.*

WHAT FILES TO CREATE AND MAINTAIN

❐ **Banking Information:** When you're online, most of the time your bank accounts will not have the full account number, and at times you need to know what that number is. If you get paper statements, put them in this file after you look them over and after you balance your account. All of the new account opening paperwork also goes in this file. Also file any business cards from bankers, letters, or other communication resulting from issues encountered at the bank.

❐ **Budget:** File a copy of your latest budget worksheet, blank copies of the worksheet, and any bills you used to create your last budget. Note: Prior to any major purchase, review your budget to ensure you can afford the new or increased payment. If you have a budget worksheet or current budgeting information, it should go in the budget file.

❐ **Car:** File your car's purchase order, loan documents, a copy of the registration (the original should be in the car's glove compartment with your address blacked out in case the car is broken into), a copy of the pink slip (the original should be kept in a fireproof, waterproof safe), insurance information if you choose, repair records, and maintenance records (oil changes, tire rotations, tire purchases, battery purchase, etc.). Note: By keeping the car's maintenance records, you can take advantage of prorated warranty programs, free tire rotations, balancing, and more; just ask about the special programs when you make a purchase. (See chapter 10 for tips on how to save on car ownership.)

❐ **Cell Phone:** Keep the contract, receipt, warranty, instruction manual, and account details. It's also helpful to cut the serial number off of the box your phone came in.

❐ **Credit:** This folder should include loan documents, credit card agreements (the one they mail you when you get the card), old credit cards you're not carrying, privacy policies, copies of your credit report, and any documentation and communication notes supporting disputes on your credit report. (See chapter 7 on credit.)

❐ **Education/School:** This file is helpful if you're actively furthering your education. If you're not in school, most of this paperwork can go in your personal file. Keep education-related items such as report cards, transcripts, awards, projects, notes from teachers, and your diploma.

❐ **Hobbies:** The list is endless here. The idea is to have a place to keep all of those little pieces of paper: ideas, articles, color swatches, you name it. Travel is one of my hobbies, so whenever I see an interesting place to go, I tear out the newspaper clipping or magazine page, or jot the info on a piece of paper, and put it in the folder. I also used this technique when I was looking for ideas to redesign my breakfast nook.

❐ **Housing:** File your rental/lease agreement, mortgage loan documents, homeowner's or renter's insurance binder, home repair records, and so on.

❏ **Goals:** File your goal worksheets, pictures, places, dreams, things you want to do. What's really cool is that when you put your written goals into this folder, you get to go back once in a while and review them…and you'll be amazed how many you've achieved. I do this twice a year. Inspiring! Write three goals on the inside of the folder; this gives you something to work toward.

❏ **Good Stuff or Accomplishments:** I talked about this in the earnings section in chapter 2, but it's nice to have a personal "good stuff" folder for things other than work. It could be notes from friends or family. It could include papers that make you feel good, emails that inspire you, accomplishments from any volunteer activities, photos from vacations, cards, letters, a note about funds you raised, work experience, and whatever makes you feel good so you can pull the file and look through it when you need a pick-me-up!

❏ **Insurance:** Pick one of the filing systems that will work for you:

  ❏ Place all of your insurance policies in one folder. If you put all of them in here, at least you'll know where they are. Remember that these companies periodically update their policies and will send you new, updated ones. If you don't have time to take out the old information, just add the new information to the folder and shred the outdated papers later. The goal is to just get it filed so you know where it is. You can do it as you go, once a year, or whatever works for you. I like the once-a-year plan. I usually do mine in January when I do my financial health checkup and go through and update my files.

❒ Have one file with a separate folder for each category: car, health homeowner's/renter's, life, dental, etc.

❒ File the insurance with the item it represents. For example, car insurance goes in your car file, homeowner's/renter's insurance goes in your housing file, health insurance goes in your work file, and so on.

❒ **Kids:** File your children's immunization records, report cards, awards, certifications, accomplishments, etc. Some of the information will be valuable to include on a college application or résumé one day.

❒ **Medical:** Be sure to keep copies of any MRIs, CT scans, blood work, and other medical information. If you move, need to have this information for another doctor, or simply need to compare your results, it will be important to have this file handy so you can get the best medical care.

❒ **Net Worth:** This is a fun file to keep up. "Net worth" may sound official, but all it is, really, is how much you're worth. It's all of your valuables minus your outstanding loans. You add up all of your assets (things of value like bank account balances, retirement, car, house, etc.), then subtract your outstanding loans (liabilities). Super easy! You can find Excel worksheets on the Internet to help you with this. It's good to do this once a year. I like to do it in January when I'm prepping for taxes.

☐ **Personal:** Put your name on it and decorate it if you want to. In addition to the receipts, warranties, and appraisals for personal items you've purchased, consider including the following: birth certificate, Social Security card, school transcripts, immunization records, old driver's license, passport (it's also a good idea to scan your passport and email it to yourself; that way, if you're traveling and your original is missing, at least you'll have a scanned copy), old photos, old work and school IDs, CPR certifications, any papers that bring back fond memories, and so on. It's also a good idea to keep a copy of everything that's in your wallet in case it's ever stolen or lost.

☐ **Pets:** Make a file for medical records, vaccinations, ID chip, and any breed registration information for your pets.

☐ **Retirement/Investment:** Keep retirement account documentation, investment statements, and even the periodic information that Social Security sends you every few years.

☐ **Supplies:** It's nice to keep some supplies on hand to reduce the need to make last-minute trips to the store for school, work, or hobby projects. Examples include computer paper, binder paper, 3x5 cards, a variety of envelope sizes, stamps, colored pens and pencils, résumé paper and envelopes, and colored paper.

❒ **Taxes:** Keep one folder for the current year. As you accumulate expenses or other things you know you'll need for tax filing, put them in this folder all year long, such as donation receipts, DMV fees, W-2s, and 1099s. That way, when it comes time to file your taxes, you'll have everything in one spot and it helps ensure you'll be able to take advantage of all the deductions you qualify for because you have the receipts and required documentation.

❒ **Trust, Will, Medical Power of Attorney:** Depending on where you are in life, you may or may not have a need for this folder right now. If you do need it, keep a copy here and tell the executor of your trust or beneficiary of your will where it is. Consider keeping the original in a fireproof, waterproof safe or in a safe deposit box at the bank. It's also important to make sure the person you've appointed as your medical power of attorney has a copy of your advanced health care directive in advance. You can mail them a copy as well as scan the document and email one to them and one to yourself; that way, if you're traveling, you can get your hands on it via the Internet.

❒ **Warranties:** If you haven't already stored your warranty booklets in a plastic bag or cupboard, store them in a folder. File all warranty booklets with a copy of the receipt attached so you can take advantage of the replacement services should the product become defective. Millions of dollars are wasted each year because people don't keep this stuff and fail to use the programs available to them!

❒ **Work/Résumés:** File all work-related items such as new-hire information or paperwork, performance reviews, certificates, thank-you notes, résumé-value project results, reminders of events, compensation details, benefits, and your previous and current résumés.

❒ **Working Files:** Whenever I'm working on a special project, I create a file so everything is in one spot, not scattered all over my desk or throughout the house. The best part is that you can create and eliminate files as needed.

BOTTOM LINE

Being financially organized is the foundation of your financial house, so make it a solid one. Taking time to build it right will do more than save you oodles of time and money. It will reduce your stress, help you reach your financial goals, and allow you to spend more time with the ones you love, doing the things you love to do.

CHAPTER NINE

Investing—Make Your Money Make Money

It feels like everywhere we turn, there's a get-rich scheme… and it always seems to leave out a few important details.

First, in order to have money to invest in anything, you must have money to begin with.

And in order to have money to begin with, you must have saved.

And the only way you can save is if you budget effectively.

And if you go the real estate route, you need to have good credit in order to get loans to purchase the real estate.

And it's very hard to manage more money than you have experience dealing with.

It's Your Money

There are all kinds of ways to make your money make money. But in order for anyone to ultimately get rich and create extreme wealth, it takes knowledge, time, discipline, and practice. I think

> **Wealth is not in your money, but in the money your money can make.**

Benjamin Franklin said it best (you know, the guy on the $100 bill): "If a man empties his purse into his head, no man can take it away from him. An investment in knowledge always pays the best interest." He also said, "Time is money." This is where your time is going to pay off big-time—because

you're investing in yourself right now by reading this book! (Good work! We need more people like you.)

Rarely are there shortcuts to making a lot of money. Being really good at anything takes time, practice, and discipline. The super rich are kind of like the quarterback on the winning team at the Super Bowl. But don't let that intimidate you. Not everyone can be that quarterback—and not everyone wants to be. That's okay! Even if you don't want to be super rich, you can still play and enjoy the game at your own level, whatever you want that to be.

 Banker's Secret

The profile of a typical millionaire might surprise you. In fact, you probably know such a person. I don't mean the extremely affluent—I'm talking about the people who have no money worries, travel when they want to, and donate to charity when they feel like it.

Their profile looks something like this:

- They always spend less than they earn.
- They pay themselves first.
- They have no debt.
- They live in the same home for years.
- They drive the same car until the wheels practically fall off.
- They don't own the latest and greatest technology.
- They understand that money can't buy happiness.
- They invest in what they know and understand that the best investment they can make is in themselves.

MAKING MONEY BABIES

Let's start at the beginning. So once you've been saving a portion of everything you earn for a while and you're living on no more than 90% of what you make, you start accumulating baskets of money—some for emergencies/stuff happens, some for when you get old, and some just to create wealth. The goal now is to make your money make money—or, as I call it, "making money babies"!

Back to the egg farmer story from chapter 3. If every day, for years, I collected 10 eggs from my hens and spent nine eggs, keeping one for myself, at some point my basket would be very full and would overflow. I'd eventually have to do something with the extra eggs I'd been saving. If I were really smart, I'd take each one of those eggs and very carefully care for them, incubating each one so the egg would hatch with another baby chick that would grow up and one day lay more eggs that would hatch and become chicks. I'd be using the combined effort of all my eggs, ensuring each one would hatch and work for me.

> **Money loves to work, but it cannot be forced into impossible earnings, so watch out for get-rich-quick schemes that promise sudden great wealth.**

So here's the goal: Your money has a baby, and your money baby has another baby, and they all go to work every day for you and produce income for you. They're working as your "employees" for your entire life, when you can no longer work or when you just want to enjoy the good life.

How does that happen? Ideally you want to create *passive income*—that is, income received on a regular basis with little effort required to maintain it (the hard work comes up front).

INVESTMENT TIPS

You should only invest in what you know. I'm not going to go into great detail here because there are simply too many different ways to put your money to work (investments). As they say, when you're ready for the lesson, your teacher will appear—so until then, keep these four things in mind:

1. Keep your money safe. Only invest it where the original amount (the principal) is safe, where you can get it back if you want.
2. Make your money earn more. You want your money to collect a reasonable rate of interest.
3. Guard your money from loss. Before you invest in anything, study it and learn about the potential risks and dangers. Be able to verbally describe what your investment is, how it works, and the risks involved.
4. Find people who are in the business of making money for profit, and carefully evaluate them and their advice.

 Banker's Secret

The best investment for you is one YOU fully understand—not necessarily the one that's being sold.

HOW TO CHOOSE AN INVESTMENT ADVISOR OR A FINANCIAL PLANNER

If you choose to find an advisor:

☐ Ask your family, friends, accountants, and lawyers for referrals. Ask people you know about people they know and trust.

☐ Ask questions—specifically, what is their experience with people like you? Know how they get paid and ask for references.

☐ Check their disciplinary action record at **finra.org**. You're looking at their ability, reputation, honesty, and ethics that show they have your best interests at heart.

INTERVIEW QUESTIONS TO ASK A PROSPECTIVE FINANCIAL ADVISOR OR FINANCIAL PLANNER

1. **Tell me about your ideal client.** _____
   Does this sound like you or who you are working to become?

   _____

2. **How long have you been practicing as a financial advisor or financial planner?** _____
   Do you feel like that is enough experience? _____

3. **Please explain _____ (stock, bond, mutual fund) concept to me.**
   Can you understand his or her explanation? _____

4. **How do you get paid?** _____

   Make sure you understand if it's a percentage of assets, hourly, fixed fee, commissioned, or a combination, and if there are additional fees.

5. **What else should I know about you and the investments you sell/represent?** _____

COMPOUND INTEREST

One of the key factors in accumulating wealth is compound interest. Here's how time can equate to money:

11% Hypothetical Return	Total Invested	Value at Age 65
Eric invested $3,000 each year from age 15-19	$15,000	$2,521,366
Beth invested $3,000 each year from age 19-27	$27,000	$2,312,620
Jamie invested $3,000 each year from age 27-65	$117,000	$1,742,478

Among other things, the graph above demonstrates the value of compound interest. You can see that Eric only set aside $15,000, yet by the time he reached 65, he had the highest investment value: $2,521,366. He was able to achieve this because he started at such an early age. You can see that Jamie, on the other hand, waited to start investing until age 27. He not only had to invest a lot more—$117,000—but the account balance totaled a lot less at $1,742,478 at age 65…$778,888 less.

Now, the above example is made using a hypothetical investment example return of 11% and is meant only for demonstration purposes. But it clearly helps you see the value of compound interest. Time is money.

 Don't Be This Guy!

A guy I knew was a pretty successful entrepreneur and was looking to expand his business. In order to do that, he needed to purchase a larger piece of property. Unfortunately, when he went out to apply for a loan, he had a really hard time getting approved because he had lots of credit inquiries and some late payments on his credit report that drove down his score—and he almost wasn't able to get the deal done. He eventually got the loan he needed, but it cost him a lot more in extra interest because of the late payments and excessive credit inquiries.

YOUR CREDIT SCORE CAN POTENTIALLY AFFECT YOUR INVESTMENTS

Even when it comes to investing, it's important to never underestimate the value of your credit score. Your credit score can play a large role in how quickly and easily you have access to things. When you have good credit, you can get things done faster and loans cost you less, allowing you the ability to close deals when others can't. When it comes to real estate deals (or any loan, for that matter), here's where your knowledge about credit will pay off big-time. When you understand and actively manage your credit score, you won't end up blowing unnecessary money on interest or potentially miss an opportunity.

If you're planning on doing any investment deals that include real estate and a mortgage, look at the credit score example below. You'll see how much a low credit score can cost you. Ouch!

30 Yr Fixed Mortgage		
FICO® Score	*APR*	*Monthly Payment*
760-850	3.768%	$1,392
700-759	3.990%	$1,431
680-699	4.167%	$1,461
660-679	4.381%	$1,499
640-659	4.811%	$1,576
620-639	5.357%	$1,677
Loan amount $300,000		

Source: Informa Research Services
Interest rates accurate as of August 25, 2014.

What this table shows, among other things, is that a person with a FICO score between 760 and 850 will have a monthly payment of $1,392 for the next 30 years, which equals $501,120 (that's $201,120). The person with a score between 620 and 639 will have a monthly payment of $1,677 for the next 30 years, which equates to a whopping $603,720 (that's $303,720 in interest). Having a lower credit score would cost this borrower an extra $102,600. Now that is a lot of money!

BOTTOM LINE

As you gain more experience with money, you will be exposed to more and more ways to invest it, so make your money work for you. Just remember the best investment you can ever make is in yourself—knowledge—and if something sounds too good to be true, it probably is. Do your own independent research, and then make an educated decision on how to invest your money.

CHAPTER TEN

Everyday Money—Spend Less and Get More

This is where we get to have fun! So meet one of the Cheapest People in America—me! Really! I was even featured in a *Reader's Digest* story, "Meet the Cheapest People in America." Now I know some people might not like being called "cheap," but I take it as a compliment. To me, it's chic to be cheap. Now don't get me wrong: I love nice things—I just don't like paying full price when I know I can get it for less if I just work the system to my advantage. I see shopping as a sport, and I love playing the financial game of life. Remember, riches are reserved for those who know and abide by the rules. That's us!

> **Never pay more than you have to—ever!**

Money is often disguised. I like to think of it as being camouflaged, or "camo cash." I love thinking about it this way because I know money is everywhere…it's just hiding from me. Every day money screams out to me when it's hiding—ka-ching, ka-ching! Dollar signs pop into my mind when I see money discussed in all kinds of things. I walk around happily singing this little song:

> *Ching-ching, it's a money thing,*
> *Ching-ching, I can do anything.*

I love singing the money song because there are a gazillion ways to save money.

Here are some of my best money-saving tips and tricks. Each tip is like a financial snack: bite-size, to the point, and designed to help you make good financial decisions. You can even have a little fun along the way.

EATING OUT

We eat out for all kinds of reasons—because we're busy, to catch up with friends, or just to enjoy the good life. How much do you think you spend on eating out each month? When you do the math (which you did in the daily spending exercise in chapter 4), it can be a really scary number. Remember the couple I worked with who were spending $900 a month on eating out, and were able to drop that number to $400 a month after putting just two of my strategies into play?

You can cut your restaurant bill by 50%! Here are some simple tips to eat, drink, and still be wealthy.

❐ **Discount gift certificates:** At restaurant.com, you can get $25 restaurant gift certificates for $10 or less. A few things you need to know: There are restrictions, like how much you need to spend, an 18% tip that may be automatically included, or a requirement to use it at specific times or days of the week. So read the fine print before you check out. When you're at the checkout screen, you'll see a little box that says either "coupon code" or "promo code." This is your cue to open another Internet browser page and do a web search for promo or discount codes for restaurant.com. Several will come up; read through them, copy and paste the best current code into the checkout box, and update your cart. By doing this you can easily save an additional 50% to 80%.

❐ **Discount coupons:** At entertainment.com, you can purchase a coupon book that has two-for-one dining coupons and other discounts for around $25 (sometimes they go on sale for $5, so sign up for alerts). This book also has discounts for groceries, entertainment, travel, and shopping. Generally there are very few restrictions on the coupons. I love using the coupons in this book to eat out with friends at work or save the second meal for later. (Be sure to tip on the full amount.)

❐ **Happy hour:** Not just for adults! Discounts await those who time it right. You'll find reduced prices on everything from slushes at Sonic Drive-In to food and adult beverages at upscale restaurants. You may have to eat at the bar, but the prices are worth it at 50% off, and sometimes the service is even better there.

❒ **Look at the bill/receipt:**

    ❒ **Errors**—Give your bill a quick look to make sure the waiter hasn't accidently charged you for someone else's meal or drink and that they have taken off any coupons you've supplied.

    ❒ **Surveys**—Often you will find online and phone surveys that offer discounts on your next visit. The restaurant wants your opinion so it can improve its service, and is willing to pay you for your time in the form of food. If you save $10 off of your next visit and it only takes you 10 minutes to complete the survey, do that six times and it's like making $60 net take-home pay per hour!

    ❒ **Tip included**—Take special note to see if they have automatically included the tip so you can avoid over-tipping.

❒ **Sign up for reward programs:** Reward programs can offer substantial discounts when you sign up via email or text. They will email you coupons and let you know when they have specials. (Note: They will send lots of emails, so you might want to set up a special email account. And texting can cost a lot, so use caution when you give your cell phone number if you don't have an unlimited texting plan.)

❒ **Social media and apps:** Discounts are everywhere and are worth checking out. Look at savings on sites like **foursquare** and **OpenTable**.

AT THE GROCERY STORE

You can reduce your grocery bill without coupons! It's astounding how much food people in the United States throw away every day, often because our food product dating system can be hard to understand.

Three dates you need to know:

1. **"Sell By" Date**—This reflects the store policy and tells the store clerk when the food must be off the shelf. This is when the store often puts items in a clearance or reduced-for-quick-sale area. This is a great way to save big, especially if you'll be using or freezing the food right away. Ask your store's management where the reduced-for-quick-sale items are located, when they put the items out, and when/if they reduce them further throughout the day.

2. **"Best By" Date**—This is all about quality guarantee: when the manufacturer guarantees the product to be at its best flavor and quality. The food is often still good after this date—it's just not at its freshest, tastiest state. Do an Internet search for "USDA food product dating." The USDA has a convenient list of storage guidelines with dates that just might surprise you, like how long eggs are good past the printed date.

3. **Expiration Date**—This is when you need to heed the warning and be very careful.

WARNING: *If food ever smells bad, looks bad, or tastes bad, don't eat it! Avoid eating food from damaged containers. Damaged containers like dented cans allow air to seep in and out and contaminate the contents, allowing bacteria to grow. And if a package is ever bulging, don't eat it; otherwise, it could be your stomach bulging when you get sick from eating it!*

More grocery store tips:

- **Dig deep**—Stores rotate their inventory, putting the food that expires the soonest up front, so dig deep. Take a few seconds to look at the dates printed on the package and find the one with the longest shelf life. This works especially well when shopping for dairy and meat products.

- **Shop the 12-week sales cycle**—Grocery stores run things on sale every 12 weeks, so if you have the storage space and the food has a 12-week shelf life, consider purchasing enough to last you 12 weeks. Items on sale are often a fraction of the regular price. Just make sure you will use the product and not allow it to go to waste.

- **Price per ounce**—This is where manufacturers and retailers try to get sneaky on us. They change the look of packaging, often reducing the size and calling it "new and improved." I love chocolate and recently noticed one candy bar company advertising its new candy bar as lighter, fluffier, and with fewer calories…*because they blew air into it!* The bar *looked* to be the same size...but they didn't pull the wool over my eyes! This is being done with everything from laundry soap to soda, so check the shelf price tag and note the *price per ounce*—it's a dead giveaway for the best deal.

❏ **Go generic**—Purchasing generic products is an easy way to save 30% or more on products, often without sacrificing quality—because generics are often made by top-name companies and labeled under store brands. I use the Costco Kirkland brand of whole coffee beans that are roasted by Starbucks, and I get them at a fraction of the cost of the Starbucks brand sitting right next to them on the shelf!

❏ **Skip the store for one week per month**—Use this week to challenge yourself to use up what you already have on the shelf and in the freezer.

SHOPPING SMART AT STORES

Retailers know there are a lot of competitors out there. They want your business, so many stores will go to great lengths to earn and keep you as a customer.

❏ **Price matching:** This strategy allows you to one-stop-shop at your favorite store and still get the best deals from all over town. If you find an item in a competitor's printed ad that is priced lower, they will match the price. All you have to do is bring the competitor's ad into the store with you when you're purchasing the item, and the competing store (if they have a price match program) will match the price. Generally the ad must be from a local competitor, the product must be currently on sale, and the product must be the identical item, brand name, quantity, and model number.

❑ **Low price guarantee:** This works much the same way as price matching. After you've purchased an item, if you find it at a lower price at another local retail competitor's store, you may be entitled to a price adjustment—which means they give you some of your money back. Policies range anywhere from 7 to 90 days. When you request an adjustment, you'll need your original receipt, proof of the new lower price, the credit card or debit card you paid with, and possibly a photo ID. It won't make sense to keep an eye out for lower prices after every single purchase, but for expensive items and for stores whose circulars you check every week, looking for price adjustment opportunities can really pay off.

 Black Friday and Cyber Monday deals may have restrictions and are often not eligible for price adjustments.

❑ **Slightly damaged goods:** When you're out shopping, ask if the store has a damaged goods section, or if you find an item you're interested in and see a small scratch or imperfection, ask if they will discount it. Don't overlook this. I've scored huge discounts (90%) on appliances, home decor, clothing, and so much more this way. Who cares if a washing machine has a dent in the side that sits up against the wall? Not me!

RECEIPTS ARE CASH, NOT TRASH

When a cashier hands you your receipt, you probably think of it as one more annoying piece of paper. Many people toss their receipts in the nearest garbage can on their way out of the store. It's particularly tempting to toss it when you paid cash and you don't even have to enter it in the checkbook. But receipts are actually cash, not trash. Here's why.

- ❒ **Coupons:** Some stores print coupons right on the receipt, or the receipt prints on a roll of paper that has coupons already printed on the back. Remember, coupons are another form of currency, like cash…they just look different!

- ❒ **Surveys:** Many stores have surveys on the bottom of their receipts so they can find out about your shopping experience. As I mentioned earlier, completing surveys is usually quick and easy, and might take 10 minutes, tops, to get $10 in products or discounts.

- ❒ **Returns:** If you have to return something, the only way to guarantee that you'll get all of your money back is to keep your receipt. Without a receipt, the retailer doesn't have to take the item back. If they do, they will likely only give you the current selling price. If the item you previously purchased is now on sale or clearance, you may only get a fraction of what you originally paid.

☐ **Rebates:** If you toss the receipt and then later discover a rebate for something you bought, you're out of luck. Most rebates require the original receipt or at least a copy of it.

☐ **Price adjustments:** If you buy something today and then it goes on sale in the immediate future (usually one to two weeks, maybe more), many retailers will refund you the difference between what you paid and the sale price. But they'll only do it if you have the original receipt.

☐ **Purchase protection:** Depending on how you paid, if the item you purchased gets lost, stolen, or damaged, you may be entitled to a refund if you have your receipt. The warranty may be extended, too (like with American Express).

☐ **Peace of mind:** You'll feel better knowing that eligible purchases can be covered against theft and accidental damage.

SHOPPING ONLINE

Nowadays people are busy, and it's hard to find time to go shopping and pick up all of the things we need and want. But thanks to modern technology, a 30-second commute to your computer offers the ultimate way to get things done, saving you money and time and reducing stress. The web is always open—no parking spots to find, no waiting in line, no lugging shopping bags around. It's all just a click or two away.

▢ **Price comparison:** Decide on what you want, then check prices on price comparison sites like pricegrabber.com, nextag.com, or bizrate.com. This helps you find the best deal on what you're looking for.

▢ **Promo codes:** Time is money—a few clicks on your computer could save you up to 90% on online purchases. Ever go to check out and see that little box that says "coupon code," "discount code," or "promo code," and wonder how you can get your hands on one? It's super easy! Open a new Internet browser page and type in "coupon/promo code" or "discount code" and the name of the site you're shopping on, and watch what pops up from your search. There will be lots of codes; read through them. You might have to try one or two to find one that works. You can also do this search for free shipping.

TIP *Keep your eyes peeled when you're shopping on a website—often times you can find a promo code or bonus stuff right in front of you when you look closely. Ka-ching!*

▢ **Partner sites:** These can quickly and easily net you additional savings or bonus rewards. If you have a card like AAA, Discover, American Express, etc., check out their website to see if they have a special page that allows you to find discounts or earn rewards with partner retailers.

▢ **Free shipping:** Check out sites like freeshipping.org to find free shipping coupon codes.

❑ **Pay the right way:** Know your rewards; some credit cards offer free shipping as a perk. Another reason to read the fine print—if you've had a credit card for a long time, it might be worth having a conversation with customer service to find out what's new and improved with your card.

❑ **Meet the minimum:** Shop with friends, family, or coworkers to meet free shipping minimums. It also works great to keep a wish list next to your computer for small items that would push you over the free-shipping minimum purchase mark.

 WARNING: *Know who you're dealing with when shopping online. Anyone can set up a website. If you're not careful, you can easily click your way around and find yourself in a bad part of cyber town.*

❑ **Read the fine print:** If you're on your phone or tablet, it can be easy to overlook this stuff—refund policy, delivery dates, etc. Restocking fees and return fees may apply and no longer make it a good deal.

❑ **Keep your packaging:** Keep the packaging for a short period of time in case you need to return the item.

❑ **Use a credit card, not a debit card:** Here's where having a credit card pays off if something goes wrong, like not receiving goods or receiving damaged goods. The Fair Credit Billing Act gives you protection for transactions you may have to dispute—and if you've used your debit card for the purchase, the cash is gone…and it's very hard to get it back or simply wait to get it back.

❐ **Resist the temptation to overspend:** Log the amounts spent shopping online in your check register, just like you do when using your debit or ATM card—just use a different color ink. That way, all of your spending is accounted for. And if you do it right, when you get your credit card bill, you can pay it off in full, avoiding going into debt and paying interest.

❐ **Look for "https":** When checking out, make sure the web address has "https"—the "s" stands for secure.

CHECK YOUR WALLET

How much money is in your wallet right now in disguise?

❐ **Student ID:** free bank accounts, movie discounts, Apple product discounts, etc.

❐ **Employee ID**: cell phone plan discounts, restaurant discounts, gym discounts

❐ **AAA card:** discounts on travel, dining, shopping and more

❐ **Credit cards:** reward program discounts, free shipping, extended warranties

❐ **Library card:** free books and music

❐ What else is in your wallet?

SAVE ON GAS

Many of us drive a lot—getting to and from school and/or work, going to the gym and the grocery store, meeting up with friends—and the price of gasoline is high. If we drive less and plan more effectively, it saves money and helps the environment. Here are a few tips.

- ❐ **Plan and combine trips:** For maximum fuel efficiency, drive to your furthest destination first so your car can warm up. Cold-engine starts burn twice as much fuel. Try to avoid peak rush hours.

- ❐ **Right-hand turns:** This gas-saving tip is what put me in the "Cheapest People in America" category in *Reader's Digest*. (By the way, I'm not crazy…I got this tip from UPS. Small things add up!) Map out your errands so you can do them without making left-hand turns. This saves wear and tear, time, and fuel. You don't have to sit in a left-hand turn lane.

- ❐ **Inflate and save:** Tire pressure is important to your car's fuel economy. According to *Consumer Reports* (love them!), riding on low tires can cost $100 a year. Low tires hurt fuel economy, cause tires to wear faster, and affect the safety, braking, and handling of your car. Check the pressure an hour after driving when the tires are cool. The proper air pressure will be on the tire or door jamb. If you have an automatic sensor, don't ignore the warning light.

- ❐ **Stop buying premium gas:** Don't buy it if you don't have to. Check the owner's manual to see if premium gas is recommended or required. If it's only recommended, you can safely use a lower octane fuel and save up to $0.20 per gallon—and you'll probably never notice a difference (unless you have a heavy foot).

SAVE ON CAR OWNERSHIP

There's nothing like driving a brand-new car with that new-car smell, the feeling of "it's all mine," and the knowledge that no one has abused it. But all of that comes with a price—a hefty price. It almost always makes more financial sense to buy a used car. Cars are better made today than they used to be. Competition among manufacturers, anticorrosion protection, and better lubricants are helping many drivers stay behind the wheel of their car for 250,000 miles or more.

If you really want to save money when you buy a car, buy a used/previously owned one. Cars depreciate (lose value) at an alarming average rate of 15% per year (depending on the make and model). That means that if you buy a brand-new car for $25,000, in three years it will only be worth about $13,750. Ouch!

Eight things to think about when buying a used car:

1. Buy a used car that's at least two or three years old (let someone else lose their money on depreciation).

2. Make sure the car has modern safety and convenience features, and has relatively low mileage for that car (my Lexus GS

400 had 100,000 miles on it when I bought it, but that's nothing for a Lexus).

3. Buy a car that has a good resell value. You can check used car values on sites like **edmunds.com, autotrader.com,** or **kbb.com** (Kelley Blue Book).

4. Buy a car with a good reliability record. My husband, Doug, really wanted an Audi A6, even after he read all of the reviews that said the car wasn't reliable and was expensive to repair. He found a used one for $10,000, bought it, and paid dearly for the next several years. He put more than $20,000 into repairs...and *finally* sold it (after my nagging) for $4,000. (Doug insists he only does stuff like this so I have something to write and talk about...thankfully he's a good sport and a great guy!) That was one expensive car. Meanwhile, I purchased a used 1998 Lexus GS 400 (yes, I know it's old, but it looks and runs great) for $13,000, have had it for six years, and have only had to do regularly scheduled maintenance. You can use the same websites listed above to research and read reviews.

5. Check insurance costs before you buy. This is especially important if you're male, are under 25, or have had tickets. Learn which cars are cheapest to insure. Middle-of-the-road sedans and minivans will be less expensive to insure. Avoid expensive, luxury, or high-performance vehicles. You can check insurance prices on a site like **insure.com.**

6. Know what the MPG (miles per gallon) of the car is.

7. Get an inspection from an independent mechanic who is ASE (Automotive Service Excellence) certified. Make sure he checks the computer system, engine, and car frame, and ensures that all safety recall work has been done.

8. Know the history of the car. You want to avoid buying a used car with hidden problems. You'll need the car's vehicle identification number (VIN) for this step. You can find it on the driver's doorjamb or on the top of the driver's dashboard (look for it from outside of the car; it's a tiny, long set of numbers). Once you have the VIN, you can check the car's history at nmvtis.gov, a Justice Department database. Make sure it wasn't totaled, stolen or damaged by flood, and also confirm the odometer reading. You can also double check the history with a private site like autocheck.com or carfax.com.

SAVE ON MAINTENANCE AND REPAIRS

Owning a car means regular maintenance and occasional repairs. This can and should be a big factor in which car you purchase. Finding the right place and person to work on your car can be a costly decision.

For example, five minutes and one phone call once saved me $200. Our Toyota Land Cruiser needed new brakes, so we took it to our regular mechanic. He called and said it would be $400. I thought that sounded expensive. So I hung up and called a Toyota dealer in town. Their quote: $200. Hmmm. I called the mechanic back and told him what I found, and he claimed his quote included rotors—that they put new rotors on every time they do a brake job. Now this is where the lesson lies: I may not know much about cars, but I do know that rotors don't need to be changed with every brake job; they can be turned. BUSTED! This guy was trying to take advantage of me, and in doing so, he lost my business forever!

❏ **Check prices:** Service and repair prices vary widely, so check around. Get at least two to three quotes: one from an independent and one from a dealer. You can ask around to find out who has a reputation of being a good, reliable, and trustworthy mechanic or shop. Be wary of shops trying to tack on work that isn't needed! You can check the owner's manual to see if the work they're suggesting really needs to be done. Sites like repairpal.com give free quotes for car repairs based on surveys of thousands of shops. Some car repair shops will also install parts bought by the customer, which could save additional money.

❏ **Prorated programs:** When it comes time to buy things like tires and batteries, look for *prorated programs.* "Prorated" means that if the item you purchase doesn't last the amount of time the warranty says it will, the company will prorate the cost of a replacement. (Divide the amount by the time you've used the item.) I had a car battery that was supposed to last five years, but it went dead after three. I went back to the same place I purchased it, and they said a new one would cost $90. I told them this one was supposed to last five years and it only lasted three. I pulled out my receipt and the price went down to $40! That receipt saved me $50! (Note: Put car repair receipts in the car folder you established (in chapter 8 on financial organization), not in the car. Leaving receipts with your personal information in the car makes you vulnerable to thieves; if your car is broken into, the thief may be able to figure out where you live and could break into your home.)

❑ **Tire lifetime service:** Many retailers also offer lifetime service on tires that include balancing, rotation, and flat repair. This can add up: A tire rotation and balance service can cost $50, and it needs to be done about every 3,000 to 5,000 miles.

BOTTOM LINE

Spending a little time before you make a purchase can save you lots of money. Every time you save $10 with a coupon or by finding a better price on something you have to buy, it means that you don't have to work for that $10.

You can make a lot out of very little. Often, it's not your resources but your *resourcefulness* that makes the difference.

So here's to enhancing your passion for finding new ways to save money. It's fun!

Enjoy the savings!

Acknowledgments

I feel like the luckiest woman in the world. We are created by the people who surround us, and I have been surrounded by many magnificent people. I would therefore like to acknowledge and thank the following:

You, the reader of this book—even if we have never met. It's people like you who have a quest for knowledge and invest in themselves, set goals and work to reach them, and take control of your financial life. It's people like you who make a difference and will be the ones to change the face of our nation's financial health.

My mom and dad for giving me life, and my sister for making every effort to love, protect, and shelter me when I was young.

The community who watched over me as a young girl. I was very lucky to have you. Your love, care, and prayers protected me at difficult times and showed me—and still show me to this day—what kindness and compassion can do.

The wonderful family who welcomed me in when I was a very young adult and taught me much about life. I appreciate your love, care, guidance, and acceptance.

My daughter, Brandi—thank you for being such a great kid and for helping me learn so much about myself and how to teach handling money as a life skill. I enjoyed our countless conversations about financial topics and how to best demonstrate each one. I know it wasn't easy being the subject of my teaching experiments. I love, admire, and respect the woman you have become.

My husband, Doug—Your constant love, support, and encouragement have filled my life so much that I am now overflowing with so much to give.

Special acknowledgment to Janice Benson, who inspired me to teach by inviting me into her classroom and helping me develop a financial and life skills program for teens. And to Mike Hale for encouraging me to jump off of the corporate cliff, for giving me a helping hand when I needed it, and for believing in me and being one of my biggest fans.

The sponsors of my financial education talks for seeing the value in what I teach, for investing in our youth, and for helping put better-educated consumers on our streets and into our workforce.

The thousands of students who attended my financial education talks and took the time to give such incredible feedback and encouragement. You showed such gratitude and appreciation to me and the sponsors of each talk.

My caring extended family, friends, and colleagues who have so generously provided support and encouraged me to follow my passion.

And finally, I want to acknowledge and thank the people who actually made this a real book: Steve Harrison and Jack Canfield for teaching me how to write a good book. Ann McIndoo for helping me get my book out of my head. Geoffrey Berwind for being an incredible coach, friend, and constant source of encouragement. Melissa Brandzel for editing, Adina Cucicov for designing the book interior, and Marcin Koziello/Grafire Studio for designing the cover.

CPSIA information can be obtained
at www.ICGtesting.com
Printed in the USA
BVHW030243140722
641719BV00005B/12

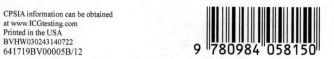